P9-CMQ-477

Blairsville High School Library

Blairsville High School Library

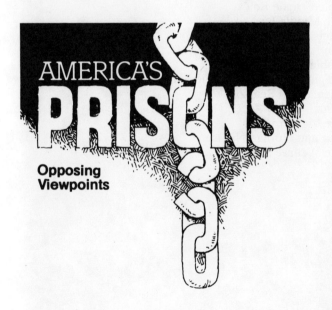

AMERICA'S
PRISONS

Opposing
Viewpoints

Other Books of Related Interest in the Opposing Viewpoints Series:

Crime & Criminals
Criminal Justice
Social Justice

Additional Books in the Opposing Viewpoints Series:

American Foreign Policy
The American Military
American Values
The Arms Race
Censorship
Central America
Chemical Dependency
Constructing a Life Philosophy
Death & Dying
The Ecology Controversy
The Energy Crisis
Male/Female Roles
The Middle East
Nuclear War
The Political Spectrum
Problems of Death
Religion and Human Experience
Science and Religion
Sexual Values
The Vietnam War
War and Human Nature
The Welfare State

Blairsville High School Library

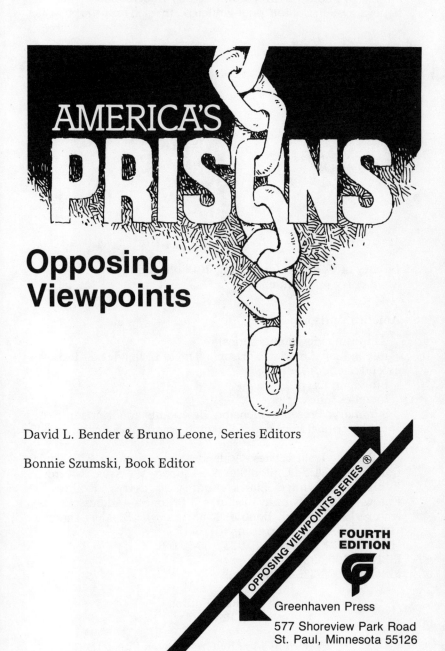

AMERICA'S PRISONS

Opposing Viewpoints

David L. Bender & Bruno Leone, Series Editors

Bonnie Szumski, Book Editor

OPPOSING VIEWPOINTS SERIES ®

FOURTH
EDITION

Greenhaven Press

577 Shoreview Park Road
St. Paul, Minnesota 55126

No part of this book may be reproduced or used in any form or by any means, electrical, mechanical or otherwise, including, but not limited to photocopy, recording or any information storage and retrieval system, without prior written permission from the publisher.

Library of Congress Cataloging-in-Publication Data
Main entry under title:

America's prisons.

(Opposing viewpoints series)
Rev. ed. of: America's prison's /David L. Bender. 3rd rev. and extended ed. c1980.
Bibliography: p.
Includes index.
Summary: Presents opposing viewpoints about prison issues. Includes critical thinking skill activities and a list of organizations to contact.
1. Prisons—United States—Addresses, essays, lectures. 2. Rehabilitation of prisoners—United States—Addresses, essays, lectures. 3. Punishment—United States—Addresses, essays, lectures. [1. Prisons—Addresses, essays, lectures. 2. Prisoners—Addresses, essays, lectures] I. Szumski, Bonnie, 1958- . II. Bender, David L., 1936- America's prisons. III. Series.
HV9471.A49 1985 365'.973 85-17168
ISBN 0-89908-350-1 (pbk.)
ISBN 0-89908-375-7 (lib. bdg.)

Fourth Edition
Revised

© Copyright 1985 by Greenhaven Press, Inc.

"Congress shall make no law...
abridging the freedom of speech,
or of the press."

First Amendment to the US Constitution

The basic foundation of our democracy is the first amendment guarantee of freedom of expression. The *Opposing Viewpoints Series* is dedicated to the concept of this basic freedom and the idea that it is more important to practice it than to enshrine it.

Contents

Why Consider Opposing Viewpoints?

"It is better to debate a question without settling it than to settle a question without debating it."

Joseph Joubert (1754-1824)

The Importance of Examining Opposing Viewpoints

The purpose of the Opposing Viewpoints Series, and this book in particular, is to present balanced, and often difficult to find, opposing points of view on complex and sensitive issues.

Probably the best way to become informed is to analyze the positions of those who are regarded as experts and well studied on issues. It is important to consider every variety of opinion in an attempt to determine the truth. Opinions from the mainstream of society should be examined. But also important are opinions that are considered radical, reactionary, or minority as well as those stigmatized by some other uncomplimentary label. An important lesson of history is the eventual acceptance of many unpopular and even despised opinions. The ideas of Socrates, Jesus, and Galileo are good examples of this.

Readers will approach this book with their own opinions on the issues debated within it. However, to have a good grasp of one's own viewpoint, it is necessary to understand the arguments of those with whom one disagrees. It can be said that those who do not completely understand their adversary's point of view do not fully understand their own.

A persuasive case for considering opposing viewpoints has been presented by John Stuart Mill in his work *On Liberty*. When examining controversial issues it may be helpful to reflect on this suggestion:

> The only way in which a human being can make some approach to knowing the whole of a subject, is by hearing what can be said about it by persons of every variety of opinion, and studying all modes in which it can be looked at by every character of mind. No wise man ever acquired his wisdom in any mode but this.

Analyzing Sources of Information

The Opposing Viewpoints books include diverse materials taken from magazines, journals, books, and newspapers, as well as statements and position papers from a wide range of individuals, organizations and governments. This broad spectrum of sources helps to develop patterns of thinking which are open to the consideration of a variety of opinions.

Pitfalls to Avoid

A pitfall to avoid in considering opposing points of view is that of regarding one's own opinion as being common sense and the most rational stance and the point of view of others as being only opinion and naturally wrong. It may be that another's opinion is correct and one's own is in error.

Another pitfall to avoid is that of closing one's mind to the opinions of those with whom one disagrees. The best way to approach a dialogue is to make one's primary purpose that of understanding the ·mind and arguments of the other person and not that of enlightening him or her with one's own solutions. More can be learned by listening than speaking.

It is my hope that after reading this book the reader will have a deeper understanding of the issues debated and will appreciate the complexity of even seemingly simple issues on which good and honest people disagree. This awareness is particularly important in a democratic society such as ours where people enter into public debate to determine the common good. Those with whom one disagrees should not necessarily be regarded as enemies, but perhaps simply as people who suggest different paths to a common goal.

Developing Basic Reading and Thinking Skills

In this book carefully edited opposing viewpoints are purposely placed back to back to create a running debate; each viewpoint is preceded by a short quotation that best expresses the author's main argument. This format instantly plunges the reader into the midst of a controversial issue and greatly aids that reader in mastering the basic skill of recognizing an author's point of view.

A number of basic skills for critical thinking are practiced in the activities that appear throughout the books in the series. Some of the skills are:

Evaluating Sources of Information   The ability to choose from among alternative sources the most reliable and accurate source in relation to a given subject.

Separating Fact from Opinion   The ability to make the basic distinction between factual statements (those that can be demonstrated or verified empirically) and statements of opinion (those that are beliefs or attitudes that cannot be proved).

Identifying Stereotypes   The ability to identify oversimplified, exaggerated descriptions (favorable or unfavorable) about people and insulting statements about racial, religious or national groups, based upon misinformation or lack of information.

Recognizing Ethnocentrism   The ability to recognize attitudes or opinions that express the view that one's own race, culture, or group is inherently superior, or those attitudes that judge another culture or group in terms of one's own.

It is important to consider opposing viewpoints and equally important to be able to critically analyze those viewpoints. The activities in this book are designed to help the reader master these thinking skills. Statements are taken from the book's viewpoints and the reader is asked to analyze them. This technique aids the reader in developing skills that not only can be applied to the viewpoints in this book, but also to situations where opinionated spokespersons comment on controversial issues. Although the activities are helpful to the solitary reader, they are most useful when the reader can benefit from the interaction of group discussion.

Using this book and others in the series should help readers develop basic reading and thinking skills. These skills should improve the reader's ability to understand what they read. Readers should be better able to separate fact from opinion, substance from rhetoric and become better consumers of information in our media-centered culture.

This volume of the Opposing Viewpoints Series does not advocate a particular point of view. Quite the contrary! The very nature of the book leaves it to the reader to formulate the opinions he or she finds most suitable. My purpose as publisher is to see that this is made possible by offering a wide range of viewpoints which are fairly presented.

David L. Bender
Publisher

Introduction

"The Law, like a good archer, should aim at the right measure of punishment."

Plato, *Laws*, XI

Prisons have become a permanent part of America's criminal justice system. As all societies have felt compelled to isolate those people who violate what is legislated as acceptable behavior, the United States has extensively developed and relied upon a prison system to perform this function. Significantly, there appears to be a correlation between social trends and ideals in America and the attitudes directed toward convicted felons. During periods of liberal reform, the enlightened treatment of prisoners and the upgrading of prison conditions were advocated. In less liberal times, the opposite was true. An examination of some of the reforms and developments that have occurred during the history of America's prison system reveals the way in which prisons and society interrelate.

Throughout the world, early prisons were horrible, unsanitary warehouses, where men, women, and children, the mentally ill, the physically old and disabled were lumped together, sometimes in one room. For example, in the British Isles during the late 18th century, "convict hulks" were used. These were abandoned or useless ships filled with prisoners. Torture, punishments, and vermin made these vessels dungeons of disease and despair. These early 'prisons,' if they can be called that, clearly had nothing but retribution in mind—constant and unending suffering with no thought as to length or purpose of sentence.

In Colonial America, prison systems also employed barbaric techniques whose main purpose was clearly revenge. Corporal punishments were most often used for persons found guilty of crimes. These were swift, painful, and supposedly corrective. Public degradation was a common chastisement for minor offenses, while hanging, burning at the stake, and breaking on the rack were among the principal punishments applied for more serious offenses. These examples clearly reflect a society which believed in the innate evil of the criminal. They exemplify a tendency to use

13

punishment for its own end, with no regard for potential rehabilitation.

Change and Progress

However, America and the rest of the world did not stagnate at this level for long. Change and progress, so obvious in other aspects of everyday life—medicine and industry among them—also affected the penal system. The predecessor of the prisons we know today was erected in 1790 in Pennsylvania. Built mainly through the reform efforts of the Quakers, its goal became not punishment, but correction, and as such, was far ahead of its time. Consistent with the Quakers' ethics, the method called for solitary confinement without work. It was assumed that offenders would be more quickly repentant and ultimately reformed if they could reflect on their crimes unhampered by distractions.

The idea that criminals could be "corrected" and that reforms in the prison system would enable criminals to return to a normal life eventually became the criteria for determining the state of prisons and the treatment of inmates. From 1870 to well into the 1940s, prisons began to employ such procedures as prisoner education, vocational training, indeterminate sentencing, and parole. These new methods clearly reflected a radical change from the inhumane treatment and fatalistic attitudes of earlier times.

Another factor significantly affected attitudes toward prison conditions and the treatment of inmates. During the 1940s, increased reliance upon and respect for the social science of psychology essentially changed the way criminologists viewed the criminal mind. Oral and written psychological tests were employed in an effort to determine the factors motivating criminal behavior. The upbringing, environment, and conscious and subconscious motives of criminals were examined to help determine not only why criminals behave as they do but also how to best deal with them. Today psychologists, and to a lesser degree, sociologists, are an integral part of America's corrections system.

Reforms May Have Increased Violence

Prison improvements have not quelled the enormous range of opinions regarding their purpose and efficacy. Today's prisons are as mired in controversy as were the prisons of the 1800s. Studies conclude that prisoner riots and violence are on the increase. Some experts have theorized that the increased number of rapes and murders that are committed among prisoners have actually been caused by reform. Progressive changes that were meant to create a more democratic environment eliminated the old, informal hierarchy that prisoners recognized and respected. This, the critics say, has been replaced by a new, less stable type of organization primarily motivated by rival gangs and racial tensions. Whether or not this theory or others is the reason for the new problems, remains unresolved. The seemingly insoluble debate has caused some to question the merit of improvements, while many reform-minded organizations and legislators continue to devote themselves unhesitatingly to bettering prison conditions.

America's Prisons: Opposing Viewpoints debates four important questions: What Is the Purpose of Prisons? How Do Prisons Affect Criminals? How Should Criminals Be Sentenced? and What Are the Alternatives to Prison? The materials included are drawn from a wide spectrum of sources and individuals. Prisoners, psychologists, victims of crime, and others are all represented in this volume. Each of the debates revolves around these related issues: How can society make prisons effective? Or more to the point, how can prisons control future criminal behavior and protect society? As readers explore these topics, the complexity and necessity of dealing with prisons make it clear that the debate will continue.

What Is the Purpose of Prisons?

AMERICA'S
PRIS NS

"When society places a person behind walls and bars it has an obligation. . . to change that person before he or she goes back into the stream of society."

Prisons Should Rehabilitate

Warren E. Burger

Many argue that prisons have become human warehouses, dehumanizing and violent places of confinement in which prisoners merely waste away, and perhaps return to society even more violent and less socially adjusted than before prison. Warren E. Burger, the chief justice of the United States Supreme Court, argues in the following viewpoint that prisons can be changed to end this pattern and become productive and rehabilitative. He believes meaningful work is needed for prisoners, in which they can take pride and feel they have a stake in society. This would eliminate the anti-social behavior that landed them in prison in the first place.

As you read, consider the following questions:

1. What are the four primary standards that must be followed in future prisons, according to Mr. Burger?
2. Does Mr. Burger believe that prisoners share society's values?
3. According to the author, how should prisoners' time be spent?

Warren E. Burger, remarks at the commencement exercises at Pace University, June 11, 1983.

Since I have been a member of the federal judiciary I have thought much and spoken often on the subject of penal and correctional institutions and those policies and practices that ought to be changed. I see this as part of the administration of justice. People go to prisons only when judges send them there and judges should have a particular concern about the effectiveness of the prisons and the correctional process, even though we have no responsibility for the management. Based on my observations as a judge for more than twenty-five years and from visiting prisons in the United States and in most of the countries of Europe—and in the Soviet Union and The People's Republic of China—I have long believed that we have not gone about the matter in the best way.

This is one of the unresolved problems on your agenda and today I will propose some changes in our approach to prisons. But before doing that, let me suggest why the subject has a special relevance, even a special urgency, right now.

Building Human Warehouses?

Our country is about to embark on a multi-billion dollar prison construction program. At least one billion dollars worth of construction is already underway. The question I raise is this: are we going to build more "human warehouses" or should we change our thinking and create institutions that are training schools and factories with fences around them where we will first train the inmates and then have them engage in useful production to prepare them for the future and to help pay for their confinement?

One thoughtful scholar of criminal justice described the state of affairs in much harsher terms than I have ever used. Four years ago he wrote this:

> Criminal justice in the United States is in a state of spreading decay . . . the direct costs of crime include loss of life and limb, loss of earnings . . . physical and mental suffering by victims and their families.

These direct losses, he continued, run into many billions of dollars annually. But indirect losses are vastly more and reach the astonishing figure of 100 billion dollars a year. These indirect costs include higher police budgets, higher private security measures, higher insurance premiums, medical expenses of the victims, and welfare payments to dependents of prisoners and victims. In the immediate future these astounding figures and the great suffering that underlies them can be reduced. This can be done by more effective law enforcement which in turn will produce a demand for more and more prison facilities. But more prisons of the kind we now have will not solve the basic problem.

Plainly, if we can divert more people from lives of crime we would benefit both those who are diverted and the potential victims. All that we have done in improved law enforcement, in new laws for mandatory minimum sentences, and changes in parole and probation practices has not prevented 30% of America's homes from being touched by crime every year. . . .

Society's Moral Obligation

On several occasions I have stated one proposition to which I have adhered to for the twenty-five years that I have worked on this problem and it is this:

> When society places a person behind walls and bars it has an obligation—a moral obligation—to do whatever can reasonably be done to change that person before he or she goes back into the stream of society.

If we had begun twenty-five, thirty-five or fifty years ago to develop the kinds of correctional programs that are appropriate for an enlightened and civilized society, the word "recidivist" might not have quite as much currency as it does today. This is not simply a matter of compassion for other human beings, it is a hard common sense matter for our own protection and our own pocketbooks.

Society Needs More Than Warehouses

We're deluding ourselves if we continue to lock people up at great cost, let them sit idle and hope that crime will just disappear. It won't. When an ex-convict returns to society unskilled, unmotivated and unaccustomed to earning a living, it's a safe bet that he will commit more crimes. New outlets for prison labor must be explored and expanded.

Gordon Mehler, *The New York Times*, July 17, 1984.

In just the past ten years prison population in America has doubled from less than 200,000 inmates to more than 400,000. This reflects, in part, the increase in crime, better law enforcement, and the imposition of longer sentences and more stringent standards of parole and probation. Budgets for law enforcement, for example, like the rates for theft insurance have skyrocketed.

Fundamental Changes Needed

If we accept the idea that the most fundamental obligation of government in a civilized society is the protection of people and homes, then we must have more effective law enforcement, but equally important, we must make fundamental changes in our prison and correctional systems. Just more stone, mortar and steel for walls and bars, will not change this melancholy picture. If we are to make progress and at the same time protect the persons and property of people and make streets and homes safe from crime, we must change our approach in dealing with people convicted of crimes. Our system provides more protection and more safeguards

19

for persons accused of crime, more appeals and more reviews than any other country in the world. But once the judicial process has run its course we seem to lose interest. The prisoner and the problem are brushed under the rug.

It is predictable that a person confined in a penal institution for two, five or ten years, and then released, yet still unable to read, write, spell or do simple arithmetic and not trained in any marketable vocational skill, will be vulnerable to returning to a life of crime. And very often the return to crime begins within weeks after release. What job opportunities are there for an unskilled, functional illiterate who has a criminal record? The recidivists who return to our prisons are like the automobiles that are called back to Detroit. What business enterprise, whether building automobiles in Detroit or ships in Norfolk, Virginia, or airplanes in Seattle, could continue with the rate of "recall" of its "products" that we see with respect to the "products" of our prisons?

The best prisons in the world, the best programs that we can devise will not totally cure this dismal problem for, like disease and war, it is one that the human race has struggled with since the beginning of organized societies. But improvements in our system can be made and the improvements will cost less in the long run than failure to make them.

New Prison Standards

I have already said that today one billion dollars in new prison facilities is actually under construction. More than thirty states have authorized construction programs, that over the next ten years will spend as much as ten billion dollars on new prison facilities.

If these programs proceed, and we must assume they will, it is imperative that there be new standards that will include the following:

(A) Conversion of prisons into places of education and training and into factories and shops for the production of goods.

(B) Repeal of statutes which limit the amount of prison industry production or the markets for such goods.

(C) Repeal of laws discriminating against the sale or transportation of prison-made goods.

(D) The leaders of business and organized labor must cooperate in programs to permit wider use of productive facilities in prisons. . . .

Prisoners Are Maladjusted

Prison inmates, by definition, are for the most part maladjusted people. From whatever cause, whether too little discipline or too much; too little security or too much; broken homes or whatever, these people lack self-esteem. They are insecure, they are at war with themselves as well as with society. They do not share the work ethic that made this country great. They did not learn, either at home or in the schools, the moral values that lead people to have respect and concern for the rights of others. But if we place that person in a factory, rather than a "warehouse," whether that factory makes ballpoint pens, hosiery, cases for watches, parts for automobiles, lawnmowers or computers; pay that person reasonable compensation, charge something for room and board, I believe we will have an improved chance to release from prison a person better able to secure gainful employment and to live a normal, productive life. If we do this, we will have a person whose self-esteem will at least have been improved so that there is a better chance that he or she can cope with life.

Making Prisoners Productive

By providing work and the chance to acquire job skills while in prison we increase the chances that inmates will become productive citizens upon release. Superior design and management can permit other programs to be more successful.

Mark W. Cannon, *Vital Speeches of the Day*, October 1, 1982.

There are exceptions of course. The destructive arrogance of the psychopath with a lack of concern for the rights of others may well be beyond the reach of any programs that prisons or treatments can provide. Our prison programs must aim chiefly at the others—those who want to change....

Costs of Confinement

Today the confinement of the 400,000 inmates of American prisons costs the taxpayers of this country, including the innocent victims of crimes, who help pay for it, more than twelve million dollars a day! I will let you convert that into billions. We need not try in one leap to copy fully the Scandinavian model of production in prison factories. We can begin with the production of machine parts for lawnmowers, automobiles, washing machines or refrigerators. This kind of limited beginning would minimize the capital investment for plant and equipment and give prisoners the opportunity to learn relatively simple skills at the outset.

We do not need the help of behavioral scientists to understand that human beings who are taught to produce useful goods for the marketplace, and to be productive are more likely to develop the self-esteem essential to a normal, integrated personality. This kind of program would provide training in skills and work habits, and replace the sense of hopelessness that is the common lot of prison inmates. Prisoners who work and study *forty-five* to *fifty-five* hours a week—as you graduates have done—are also less prone to violent

21

prison conduct. Prisoners given a *stake* in society, and in the future, are more likely to avoid being part of the "recall" process that today sends thousands of repeat offenders back to prisons each year . . . .

But I would say that every prisoner should be "induced" to cooperate by the same methods that are employed in many other areas. Life is filled with rewards for cooperation and penalties for noncooperation. Prison sentences are shortened and privileges are given to prisoners who cooperate. What I urge are programs in which the inmate can earn and learn his way to freedom and the opportunity for a new life.

Rewards and Punishments

Opportunities for rewards and punishments permeate the lives of all free people and these opportunities should not be denied to prison inmates. At the core of the American private enterprise system is the idea that good performance is rewarded and poor performance is not. So I say we can induce inmates to cooperate in education and in production. A reasonable limit is that they should not be made to study more or work longer hours for example, than students at Pace University must work to earn a degree! Surely it would not be rational to settle for less. I can hardly believe that anyone would seriously suggest that prisoners should be treated with less discipline than the young men and women in the colleges of America.

"By the two most common standards used to rationalize the existence of [them]—rehabilitating the criminal and deterring crime—[prisons] don't work."

Prisons Cannot Rehabilitate

Michael A. Kroll

Michael A. Kroll is a former Washington director of the National Moratorium on Prison Construction. He is also a contributing editor of Pacific News Service. Research for this viewpoint was supported by grants from the Fund for Investigative Journalism and the Playboy Foundation. Mr. Kroll argues that prisons have no economic incentive to make them more rehabilitative. Prisons provide profits for corporations as diverse as Coca Cola and tear gas grenade makers. Moreover, they employ thousands of state and federal workers and many architectural firms. All of these groups, Mr. Kroll contends, have a stake in making sure prisoners remain in prison.

As you read, consider the following questions:

1. Why does the author believe that in actual operation, the purpose of prison is in direct conflict with rehabilitation?
2. Why will prison job programs and rehabilitation programs not work, according to the author?
3. What is the author's solution?

Michael A. Kroll, "Prisons for Profit," *The Progressive*, September 1984. Reprinted by permission from *The Progressive*, 409 East Main Street, Madison, Wisconsin 53703. Copyright © 1984, The Progressive, Inc.

When Richard Nixon called the American prison system "a convincing case of failure" fifteen years ago, he was restating an oft-repeated and voluminously documented fact: By the two most common standards used to rationalize the existence of prisons—rehabilitating the criminal and deterring crime—they don't work.

But from another vantage point, from the perspective of those whose livelihoods depend on prisons, the system is an unqualified success. "Prisoners are commodities, and a profit must be realized from commodities," says Norman Nusser, who has served seventeen years of his twenty-to-forty-year sentence for burglaries in Pennsylvania. "A lot of 'good guys' make an easy living off the misery of us 'bad guys.'"

More than 432,000 Americans are being held in state and Federal prisons—a figure that has increased by 80,000 in the past two years. California leads the nation with 37,000 inmates, up 74 per cent since the beginning of this decade. All told, the combined U.S. prison and jail population exceeds 644,000, making our national incarceration rate third in the industrial world behind the Soviet Union and South Africa.

Prison Cities

The vast number of American prisoners makes up a community more populous than St. Louis, Boston, Seattle, or Denver—even more populous than Alaska, Wyoming, Vermont, or Delaware. It is an invisible nation larger than twenty members of the United Nations.

And it is a gold mine to private business. "In Illinois, where the inmate total has more than doubled in a decade, officials call corrections the state's major growth industry," *U.S. News & World Report* recently noted.

Consider the stake of architects. States spent $133 million for prison construction and expansion in 1980, according to the Justice Department. In 1981, that expenditure rose to $348 million, and in 1982, to almost $800 million.

The National Moratorium on Prison Construction, a project of the Unitarian Universalist Service Committee, estimates that more than 800 jails and prisons are on the drawing board or being built—at a projected cost of $6 billion. Upwards of 100 firms specialize in prison architecture, says the chairman of the American Institute of Architecture's criminal justice committee.

The competition drove one Michigan entrepreneur to open a new line: "do-it-yourself, easy-to-assemble portable jails." "The gamble is so fantastic," he explains, "that once this thing goes, we're talking about scads and scads of money."

Though not an architect, Robert Britton also recognized the opportunities offered by prisons. In 1981, as Alabama Prison Commissioner, he urged a massive ten-year construction program for his state: completion of two prisons and "at least six more

1,000-man institutions." Britton then left his post to head a medical firm that serves Alabama's prisons. "I've always wondered what the corporate world is like," he said.

Corporations Within Prisons

Inside prisons, the corporate world includes Aerko International's Mister Clear Out ("The state of the art in tear gas hand grenades especially designed for indoor use"); the Peerless Handcuff ("A major breakthrough in cuff design"); Disposable Waste Systems' Muffin Monster ("It will grind up into small pieces all the things that inmates put down toilets"); Servomation, a food distribution company ("Justice is served"), and Coca-Cola ("Time goes better with Coke").

Because the individual's failure is the industry's success, some inmates have concluded that the enervation they suffer is no accident. They say high recidivism—the rate at which ex-convicts return to prison—is in the best interest of corrections bureaucrats and companies.

"Our system is in league with the criminal," asserts Nusser. "Our

"No prisoner was ever more rehabilitated. In over fifty years of crime, he's been rehabilitated 16 times."

© Gauerke/Rothco

prisons are reducing the prisoners' capacity for being human. We are ensuring—underwriting—a future increase of victims of crime."

"They have no interest in reducing crime," says Michael Alston, serving a ten-to-twenty-year stretch for bank robbery in Connecticut's maximum-security prison at Somers. "They earn their living off us."

"Just think what a catastrophe it would cause if all cons across the country decided never to commit another crime," says Henry Abernathy, serving a life sentence for a Texas bank robbery. "Think of how many different hands I go through from the time I'm arrested. Lots of dollars and lots of jobs. We are their bread and butter."

"Just the title, 'Department of Corrections,' is a misnomer," declares Richard Cepulonis, an inmate at the maximum-security prison in Walpole, Massachusetts. "They don't correct anything. They debilitate people and return them to a competitive society knowing they can't compete. They vilify self-determination and label those who seek to habilitate themselves as seditious malcontents." . . .

Rehabilitation a Gimmick

Prisoners have come to view so-called rehabilitation programs as gimmicks to bring money into the institutions. Henry Abernathy, now incarcerated at the Federal penitentiary in Terre Haute, Indiana, once did time in Texas, where he took a course in electronics offered by Lee College in Baytown. "On my diploma it states that I am a 'distinguished scholar' with a straight-A grade average," he says, "but I can't even take the back off a radio. We were never allowed to because the officials said once we got a radio or television working, we would just want to sit around all day and listen or watch." . . .

Brittian Thornton, a convict at California's San Quentin Prison, says, "Genuine self-improvement is actively resisted by the system. The name of the game is different, but the game is the same: 'Give the nigger a book . . . .' It goes right back to slavery."

Jails for Profit

Though the dollar has helped warp the prisons, more and more experts are touting the profit motive as a way to straighten them out. "It's time to get government out of the prison business," says Peter Greenwood, who directs the Rand Corporation's criminal justice program. "When you're looking for innovation, you don't look to government, you look to business."

For-profit jails are being opened in several states. In California, a retired parole officer, Ted Nissen, runs a detention center for illegal immigrants. The Federal Government pays Nissen $23 a day per inmate for his services. "I've got to think like Colonel Sanders," he says. "I'll try anything. If it works and I make a profit, I'll stick with it."

But even where prisons are financed with public money—and presumably with public policy in mind—economic concerns can be paramount. State officials planning new prisons often find the most favorable response in areas devastated by unemployment.

If the promise of a steady payroll is not enough to persuade residents to accept a prison in their neighborhood, E.F. Hutton & Company, Inc., offers "Exciting New Ways to Finance Jails"—ways that avoid the voters. "As a nation," begins the Hutton promotional literature, "we have an unprecedented need to acquire new jails and prisons." The desirability of more prisons is assumed; the clear advantage of fewer prisoners is ignored.

Profit Disguised as Rehabilitation

Let a spade be a spade. When prisons are turned into "factories and shops for the production of goods," it will not be for our benefit, rather for the benefit of those vested interests concerned only with turning a profit off our sweat. Today we are as despised as slaves; tomorrow we will be used as such.

Wilbert Rideau and Billy Sinclair, *Fortune News*, Autumn 1983.

One state, recognizing the power of economic self-interest, has used it to move away from an expanding prison industry, at least in the area of juvenile justice.

When Jerome Miller took over the juvenile justice system of Massachusetts in 1969, the budget he inherited was a typical one: 95 per cent was allocated to institutional upkeep (largely staff salaries), while 5 per cent went to community programs. By the time he left in 1974, the proportions were exactly reversed.

Expand Community Program Budget

Miller relied on staff attrition to move money from institutional budgets to alternative programs. He was able to close the state's "training schools" and expand a variety of community programs, including one-on-one supervision. When he arrived, 1,500 youngsters were in secure lock-up, a number comparable to other states. Now there are fewer than seventy juveniles behind bars in Massachusetts.

Moreover, the juvenile crime rate in Massachusetts is declining and stands lower than that of other Eastern states. The percentage of adult inmates who are alumni of the juvenile justice system has dramatically declined, from 46 in 1969 to 19 today.

"The mechanism to move from locked institutions to community programs is available in most state budgets," says Miller, who currently runs the National Center on Institutions and Alternatives in Washington, D.C. "It's about a five-year process. But it requires taking some political risks."

Miller's success in Massachusetts suggests that those risks are not as great as one might expect. During the tenure of conservative Governor Edward King, an attempt was made to revert to the old "lock 'em up" policies that serve politicians so well. But the communities themselves resisted the move—and that is the genius of Miller's achievement. With the state's dollars now vested in the community, a powerful lobby against prisons has been built.

Following the lead of Massachusetts, Utah has reduced the number of juveniles behind bars from 400 to forty-four in the last five years. According to Russell VanVleet, who leads the effort, the change in Utah's system is symbolized by the conversion of the old Youth Development Center. "The campus that stood for abuse and institutional evil has been renovated and converted to an area vocational center," he says.

Like Miller, VanVleet believes that any state can move away from incarceration if it chooses to do so. "It is only a question of commitment," he says, "commitment that is philosophical and political."

But building such a commitment requires an understanding of what angers the prisoners themselves: the role of the profit motive in perpetuating a system that everyone acknowledges is a failure.

Everyone, that is, except the folks who make a buck when liberty is denied.

"The most desirable penal policy is that of just punishment, the swift punishing of blameworthy behavior."

Prisons Should Punish

Francis T. Murphy

Prisons were originally constructed as a humane alternative to the public floggings and executions that were originally used to punish criminals. They were to be havens where prisoners could do hard labor and repent their crimes in solitude. Francis T. Murphy, a presiding justice of the appellate division of the Supreme Court, argues in the following viewpoint that prisons have lost this original purpose. Criminals have broken society's moral rules, he concludes, and prison should effectively punish them for this infraction.

As you read, consider the following questions:

1. What factors does the author cite to prove the public no longer believes that criminal behavior can be changed?
2. Why, according to the author, should punishment be the goal of prison?
3. What standards must people hold themselves to, according to the author?

Francis T. Murphy, "Moral Accountability and the Rehabilitative Ideal," *New York State Bar Journal*, January 1984. Reprinted with permission. Copyright 1984, New York State Bar Association.

When a man is sentenced and led from courtroom to prison, two statements have been made as the door closes behind him. The judge has spoken to his crime, and society has spoken of how it will deal with him. Embedded in these statements is a fascinating complex of ideas about the nature of man, morality, law and politics.

Prior to the 1800's, the prison system was unknown. Society's answer to the felon was usually given at the end of a rope or the swing of an axe. In imposing sentence, a judge was virtually a clerk, for he had no discretion in the matter. He simply sent the defendant to a death commanded by law.

During the first half of the 1800's, however, a confluence of ideas and political events produced the prison in America. So unusual was the idea of the prison that Europeans came to America in order to visit prisons and record what they saw.

The Idea of Prisons

How did the idea of the prison originate? In part, the prison was a humane answer to the criminal. Hanging a man for stealing a spoon or forging a note seemed immoral. In great part, the prison was an economic indulgence, for prior to the Industrial Revolution society could not have afforded prisons. Yet, lying behind humane motives and the new economy was a belief that included much more than the prison. The first half of the 1800's was an age of reform. Belief in the perfectibility of human beings and in the improvement of their social institutions was prevalent. In America and Europe a liberalism traceable to thinkers like Locke and Erasmus, to the Renaissance and ancient Greece, had as its central principle that to every question there was a rational answer, that man was able to discover rational solutions to his problems, and when thus enlightened he could live in a harmonious society. It was natural that a belief of that magnitude, infused into economic and social problems of every kind, and joined with a humanitarian spirit and the new, industrial wealth, would inhibit the tying of the rope and the swinging of the axe. Thus it was that the first half of the 1800's introduced in America not only the prison as a place for punishment and deterrence, but the prison as a place for the rehabilitative ideal, today condemned by many as the right idea in the wrong place.

The Rehabilitative Ideal

A usable definition of the rehabilitative ideal is that a primary purpose of penal treatment is the changing of the character and behavior of the prisoner in order to protect society and to help him. It is an idea that has attracted groups who march to the beat of very different drums. It has attracted those who think of crime as an individual's moral failure, or as an evil caused by corrupt social institutions, or as an entry in the printout of a prisoner's genetic program. Accordingly, the rehabilitative ideal has elicited different

30

means—extending from the early 1800's imposition of absolute silence upon all prisoners in New York, and the unrelieved solitary confinement of all prisoners in Pennsylvania, to the twentieth century's faith in therapeutic interventions, such as the promoting of literacy, the teaching of vocational skills, the use of psychotherapy, and the less popular surgical removal of brain tissue. All of these means have one thing in common. Each has failed as a reliable rehabilitative technique and each, ironically, has today drawn public anger not upon those working in the rehabilitative disciplines, but upon very visible judges few of whom, if any, purport to be competent in any rehabilitative skill. Indeed, it is an anger that has a sharp edge, for though judges observe a traditional silence when accused of failing to rehabilitate the imprisoned, judges nevertheless have legislatively or constitutionally been drawn within the range of public attack in other areas of the rehabilitative ideal—sentencing discretion, the indeterminate sentence, probation, parole, and prison conditions.

Punishment Advances Human Dignity

But why punish [criminals]?. . . The answer, I think, is clear: We want to punish them in order *to pay them back*. We think they must be made to pay for their crimes with their lives, and we think that we, the survivors of the world they violated, may legitimately exact that payment because we, too, are their victims. By punishing them, we demonstrate that there are laws that bind men across generations as well as across (and within) nations, that we are not simply isolated individuals, each pursuing his selfish interests and connected with others by a mere contract to live and let live.

Walter Berns, *For Capital Punishment,* 1979.

Notwithstanding that the rehabilitative ideal never actually dominated the criminal justice system as a value prior to punishment and deterrence, it was generally believed by the public and the Bench that it had that primacy. In any case, substantial defections from that ideal began about twenty years ago, not only among editorial writers and politicians but among scholars as well. Today, the ideal is incanted solemnly at sentence, but even then neither Bench nor counsel discuss it.

Why has the rehabilitative ideal depreciated so sharply? The answer must be traceable to ideas that drain belief in the notion of the mutability of human character and behavior. I will point to several of them.

The nineteenth century belief in the simplicity and perfectibility of human nature has been profoundly shaken by the Freudian revolution, to say nothing of the unprecedented savagery of the twentieth century. There is in America a continuing and almost apocalyptic increase in crime, notwithstanding that our average sentence is the longest in the western world. Inevitably, a sense of helplessness, a foreboding of a collapse of public order is present at every dinner table. As for confidence in the utility of traditional therapeutic means, it has all but vanished. Indeed, it is generally accepted that a rehabilitative technique of any kind is yet to be discovered. Belief in the power of the public educational system to perform its simplest objective has been lost, hence the claims of education are not received as once they were. There has been a profound depression in the structure and authority of the family, and with it a decline of those family virtues associated with rehabilitation. A pervasive pessimism, an almost open contempt, for government has seeped into the public mind. A new mentality has arisen, markedly anti-intellectual in orientation, disclosing in American culture a sense of dependency, a seeking out of comfort and self-awareness, a flight from pain and personal responsibility. Moral passion has not declined. It has disappeared. These social facts are fragments of deeper changes which strikingly distinguish the major political movements of the twentieth century from those of the nineteenth. As Isaiah Berlin has observed, two devastating elements, traceable to Freud or Marx, have united in the political movements of the twentieth century. One is the idea of unconscious and irrational influences that outweigh reason in explaining human conduct. The other is the idea that answers to problems exist not in rational solutions but in the extinguishing of the problems by means other than thought. So it is that the rehabilitative ideal, congenial to the essentially intellectual age of reform of the early 1800's, has depreciated with the twentieth century's devaluation of the intellect and the will. Looking back over the past two centuries, we see that science, as a new way of knowing, not only promised to augment man's power but dramatically delivered on that promise. The power it delivered, however, proved to be over nature only. It did not increase our power over ourselves to become better people. It has left man unchanged, sitting, as it were, in the evening of his life in a warehouse filled with his technology.

Prisons Are for Punishment

We are thus living at a critical point in the shaping of an American penal policy. We could increase penal sanctions by matching brutality for brutality, but ethics and utility argue against it. In any case, a political consensus fortunately does not support what is essentially a regressive, primitive gesture. Equally without a political consensus are programs for social reforms directed at what some think to be causes of crime—unemployment, racial discrimination, poor housing. Whether such conditions cause crime is disputed and, in any case, a penal policy is too narrow a platform upon which a plan of social reform can be based.

In my opinion, the most desirable penal policy is that of just punishment, the swift punishing of blameworthy behavior to the degree of the offender's culpability. By such a policy we reaffirm the reality of moral values. Thus we answer those who challenge the conception of man's moral responsibility. Thus we create hope in a future based upon ancient moral truths from which so many have drifted into a night of philosophical neutrality.

Prisons, Rehabilitation Don't Mix

The idea of just punishment has a wide consensus. It is a statement of a natural, moral intuition. It declares the moral autonomy of man without which all value systems are bound to be anarchic. It recaptures the lost community of moral and legal elements which once characterized crime and punishment, and without which a society loses its stability. As for the rehabilitative ideal, it should be stripped of its pretentiousness, if not of its very name. It is a hope of changing behavior, and nothing more. It is a goal, not a reality. In prison it should be directed at objectives that can be realized, particularly the avoidance of the deformative influences of prison life. Efforts at rehabilitation might well be concentrated at the offender outside of the prison setting, the one place where rehabilitation might have a fair chance of accomplishment. Surely rehabilitation is unlikely in prisons in which minimum standards of personal safety, health, and humane treatment are often violated.

Punishing the Criminal

We should do better to look at the [prison] problem from a just deserts point of view and ask ourselves, do not these criminals who have long records and have committed unspeakable crimes, deserve to be punished more severely, and in a way that is appropriate to their crimes? We do not seek to "cure" the criminal, but rather for him to atone for his crime. The term of imprisonment must be one that keeps up front, very clearly in view, that the criminal is there to *be punished*, to have the judge's sentence erased from his forehead, just as was the burden of the seven sins erased from that of Dante as he progressed through each stage of Purgatory.

Graeme R. Newman, *Just and Painful*, 1983.

Indeed one cannot leave the literature of penology without the conviction that, if he were required to design a place in which the behavior of a man could never be improved, he would draw the walled, maximum security prison, very much like those into which men were led for rehabilitation in the early 1800's and are kept until this very day.

This time in which we live need not be an age of cynicism and despair. There is no principle that compels us to accept the philosophical debris of history. This time can, if we would but will it, be an age in which the fixed human values of Western civilization are brought back into their natural ascendancy. They who believe that man is not truly free, and hence not truly responsible, who market man as a rational animal without free will, who recognize neither good nor evil but only what is personally useful or harmful, who find the rule of right and wrong only in the current opinion of men, all these are strangers in the West. The values of Western civilization are ultimately the standards of men who hold themselves accountable for their moral acts. Upon that accountability all social institutions rise and fall.

"When measured against the probable reduction in crime, prolonged incarceration is not worth the financial burden it imposes on state and local governments."

Punishment Does Not Work

Richard Moran

Richard Moran, a professor of criminology at Mount Holyoke College, argues that using prisons to get tough with criminals and as punishment is not working. While offering no solution to the prison problem, Mr. Moran believes that the sheer magnitude of crimes committed makes it impossible to use prison as a punishment for all of them.

As you read, consider the following questions:

1. Is the criminal population increasing or decreasing, according to the author?
2. Why are most prisoners released early, according to the author?
3. How much does the author claim it costs to keep one prisoner in prison for one year?

Richard Moran, "More Crime and Less Punishment," *Newsweek*, May 7, 1984. Copyright 1984 by Newsweek, Inc. All rights reserved. Reprinted by permission.

If you are looking for an explanation of why we don't get tough with criminals, you need only look at the numbers. Each year almost a third of the households in America are victimized by violence or theft. This amounts to more than 41 million crimes, many more than we have the capacity to punish. There are also too many criminals. The best estimates suggest that 36 million to 40 million people or 16 to 18 percent of the U.S. population have arrest records for nontraffic offenses. We already have 2.4 million people under some form of correctional supervision, 412,000 of them locked away in a prison cell. We don't have room for any more!

The painful fact is that the more crime there is the less we are able to punish it. This is why the certainty and severity of punishment must go down when the crime rate goes up. Countries like Saudi Arabia can afford to mete out harsh punishments precisely because they have so little crime. But can we afford to cut off the hands of those who committed more than 35 million property crimes each year? Can we send them to prison? Can we execute more than 22,000 murderers?

Punishment and Crime

We need to think about the relationship between punishment and crime in a new way. A decade of sophisticated research has failed to provide clear and convincing evidence that the threat of punishment influences the rate of most major crimes committed. We assume that punishment deters crime, but it just might be the other way around. It just might be that crime deters punishment: that there is so much crime that it simply cannot be punished.

This is the situation we find ourselves in today. Just as the decline in the number of high-school graduates has made it easier to gain admission to the college of one's choice, the gradual increase in the criminal population has made it more difficult to get into prison. While elite colleges and universities have held the line on standards of admissions, some of the most "exclusive" prisons now require about five prior felony convictions before an inmate is accepted into their correctional program. Our current crop of prisoners is an elite group, on the whole much more serious offenders than those who inhabited Alcatraz during its heyday.

As Powerless as Parents

Given the reality of the numbers it makes little sense to blame the police, judges or correctional personnel for being soft on criminals. There is not much else they can do. The police can't find most criminals and those they find are difficult and costly to convict. Those convicted can't all be sent to prison. The social fact is that we cannot afford to do nothing about crime. The practical reality is that there is very little the police, courts or prisons can do about the crime problem. The criminal-justice system must then become as powerless as a parent who has charge of hundreds of teen-age children and who is nonetheless expected to answer the TV message: "It's 10 o'clock! Do you know where your children are?"

A few statistics from the Justice Department's recent "Report to the Nation on Crime and Justice" illustrate my point. Of every 100 felonies committed in America, only 33 are actually reported to the police. Of the 33 reported, about 6 are cleared by arrest. Of the six arrested, only three are prosecuted and convicted. The others are rejected or dismissed due to evidence or witness problems or diverted into a treatment program. Of the three convicted, only one is sent to prison. The other two are placed on probation or some form of supervision. Of the select few sent to prison, more than half receive a maximum sentence of five years. The average inmate, however, graduates into a community-based program in about two years. Most prisoners gain early release not because parole boards are soft on crime, but because it is much cheaper to supervise a criminal in the community. And, of course, prison officials must make room for the new entering class of recruits sent almost daily from the courts.

Prisons Not the Answer

We could, of course, get tough with the people we already have in prison and keep them locked up for longer periods of time. Yet when measured against the probable reduction in crime, prolonged incarceration is not worth the financial burden it imposes on state and local governments who pay the bulk of criminal-justice costs. Besides, those states that have tried to gain voter approval for bonds to build new prisons often discover that the public is unwilling to pay for prison construction.

Forget the Punishment Thing

Forget the punishment thing and all your troubles are easy. You're not busy beating the hell out of him because he's bad and you're good; you're trying to decide what's best for the community, and what's good for this individual. I don't want the institution paid for by my money to be entertaining itself burning him with hot irons.

Karl Menninger, *Corrections Magazine*, August 1981.

And if it were willing to pay, prolonged incarceration may not be effective in reducing crime. In 1981, 124,000 convicts were released from prison. If we had kept them in jail for an additional year, how much crime would have been prevented? While it is not possible to know the true amount of crime committed by people released from prison in any given year, we do know the extent to which those under parole are reconfined for major crime convictions. This number is a surprisingly low 6 percent (after three years it rises to only 11 percent). Even if released prisoners commit an average of two crimes each, this would amount to only 15,000 crimes prevented: a drop in the bucket when measured against the 41 million crimes committed annually.

Prison Is Expensive

More time spent in prison is also more expensive. The best estimates are that it costs an average of $13,000 to keep a person in prison for one year. If we had a place to keep the 124,000 released prisoners, it would have cost us $1.6 billion to prevent 15,000 crimes. This works out to more than $100,000 per crime prevented. But there is more. With the average cost of prison construction running around $50,000 per bed, it would cost more than $6 billion to build the necessary cells. The first-year operating cost would be $150,000 per crime prevented, worth it if the victim were you or me, but much too expensive to be feasible as a national policy.

Faced with the reality of the numbers, I will not be so foolish as to suggest a solution to the crime problem. My contribution to the public debate begins and ends with this simple observation: getting tough with criminals is not the answer.

"Our criminal justice system seems to have forgotten that its goal is to protect honest citizens from criminals."

Prisons Are for Society's Protection

Allan C. Brownfeld

Allan C. Brownfeld is a nationally syndicated columnist. He is published widely in conservative newspapers and journals. In the following viewpoint, Mr. Brownfeld expresses his anger at the criminal justice system for releasing criminals early only to have them prey on society and victimize more innocent people. A prison's primary purpose should be to take criminals off the streets.

As you read, consider the following questions:

1. How does the author believe that parole and probation harm the general public?
2. Mr. Brownfeld cites some rather shocking crime statistics. What do these crime statistics represent, according to the author?
3. According to the author, has psychological treatment of prisoners helped society?

Allan C. Brownfeld, "Putting Killers on the Streets," *The Washington Times,* April 20, 1984. Reprinted with the author's permission.

Recently, in a typical case, a man free on parole after a manslaughter conviction was arrested and charged with murdering a New York City Police officer and wounding two others. Twenty-four-year-old George Acosta had a long history of arrests, beginning when he was 16 years old. The last two came while he was on parole after serving three years of a 5-to-15 year sentence in the 1977 slaying of an 18 year old youth in a Bronx social club. Bronx District Attorney Maio Merola described Acosta as "a career criminal."

Mr. Acosta was paroled in August 1982, arrested on a gun possession charge the next January and then arrested on a burglary charge. He pleaded guilty to burglary and served a four-month sentence. But his parole on the manslaughter sentence remained in effect. He was free to kill again. And he did.

In another much publicized case in California Theodore Streleski was paroled after serving only five years for murder. On a summer day in 1978, Streleski, then a Stanford University graduate student, crept silently into the office of his faculty adviser and bludgeoned him to death with a hammer. After taping the victim's head inside a plastic bag, he calmly placed a sign on the door saying "No Office Hours Today." He told police that he had plotted the killing of Professor Karel de Leeuw over a period of years as "a political statement" against the university's treatment of graduate students and as "a logically and morally correct action."

Under California's 1976 determinate sentencing law, Streleski received the maximum sentence of seven years with one additional year for the use of a deadly weapon—hardly a sentence commensurate with the crime. After serving two-thirds of that time, according to the law, he had to be paroled. He was arrested three hours after being released for refusing to abide by the terms of the parole—fortunately before he killed again, which he has said he would do.

Releasing Threats to Society

Clearly, prison systems throughout the U.S. are releasing prisoners who are obvious threats to society. In eleven states, including California, parole release has now been abolished for most offenders in favor of a fixed or "determinate" sentencing system. Under it, a judge must impose punishment from a narrow range of options set by the legislature or some administrative body, and an offender must serve all of the sentence, minus time off for good behavior. Such states have eliminated the old "one-to-20-year" sentences, which left parole boards to decide the real length of time.

In recent years, New York's parole commissioners have annually considered the cases of 15,000 inmates seeking early release from prison. Last year, the board decided to parole 8,300 inmates, with two-thirds being released to New York City's streets—including George Acosta. "Right now we have judges supposedly doing the

40

IT'S TIME TO TAKE A SECOND LOOK!..

©Dobbins/Rothco

sentencing," said Lawrence T. Kurlander, Governor Mario Cuomo's criminal justice coordinator, "but the real sentencing is being done by the Parole Board within the confines of prison walls, by what criteria we don't know."

The president of the United Probation Officer's Association in New York, Wallace Cheatham, declares: "A significant number of offenders on probation are every day committing robberies, assaults, murders and other serious crimes. One-third of all offenders being placed on probation instead of being supervised, merely have to call in once a month to a clerk. The unconscionable high case loads means that anyone placed on probation in New York City receives little or no supervision. Almost fifty per cent of offenders placed on probation are re-arrested within the first eight months of their sentence."

Our criminal justice system seems to have forgotten that its goal is to protect honest citizens from criminals—and that men and women must be held responsible for their actions. For too long, the alleged "well-being" of the perpetrators of crime seems to have been of more concern than the protection of society. What has been the result of this approach? Our crime rate is by far the highest in the industrial world. Violent crimes of assault or rape and of burglary now touch more than 10 per cent of U.S. households. If the lesser crime of larceny is included, the number of households involved is 30 per cent. The chances of being a victim of violent crime nearly tripled in the last 25 years, as did the possibility of being the victim of a serious crime such as burglary or auto theft. According to the F.B.I.'s Crime Clock, one crime is committed every two seconds, one violent crime every twenty-four seconds, one murder every 23 minutes, one rape every six minutes.

While crime has increased, our criminal justice system has made it easier for perpetrators to escape punishment. For every 500 serious crimes, just 20 adults and 5 juveniles on average, are sent to jail—a ratio of 1 in 20. Of some 2 million serious criminal cases filed each year, only 1 in 5 actually goes to trial. In New York State in 1980, of the 130,000 men and women arrested for felonies, only about 8,000 actually went to prison. Sociologists calculate that if the robbery rate in large cities continues to grow as it did between 1962 and 1974, by the year 2024 each man, woman and child in a large city would be robbed by force or threat of force 2.3 times per year.

Insightful Rapists

Rather than putting murderers and rapists in prison—and preventing them from murdering and raping again—we seek to "treat" their alleged "problems." In his important book, "Inside The Criminal Mind," psychologist Stanton E. Samenow recalls his work with Dr. Samuel Yochelson at St. Elizabeth's Hospital: "Dr. Yochelson treated rapists using psychoanalytic concepts and techniques, and what he found was, he then had rapists with psychiatric insight." Criminals, Dr. Samenow points out, love the Freudian approach: "They learn to fool the psychiatrists by playing the psychiatric game of mouthing insights. . . . By taking the position that the criminal is a victim, society has provided him with excuses and supported his contention that he is not to blame."

To argue that men are not responsible for what they do is to deny all of us our humanity. We should recall the point made by G.K. Chesterton in his classic work, "Orthodoxy": "The fallacy to the torrent of model talk about treating crime as a disease, about making a prison merely a hygienic environment like a hospital, of healing sin by slow scientific methods . . . is that evil is a matter of active choice, whereas disease is not."

"Prisons are a massive deception: seeming to 'protect,' they engender hostility and rage among all who are locked into the system."

Prisons Cannot Protect Society

Prison Research Education Action Project

The Prison Research Education Action Project (PREAP) designs and distributes education/action tools for use by those working for the abolition of prisons. In the following viewpoint, PREAP attacks the notion that prisons protect society. The organization argues that prisons themselves are responsible for turning criminals into dangerous and vengeful beings with a bloodthirsty need to take their hatred out on society once they are released.

As you read, consider the following questions:

1. What types of criminals get caught, according to the author?
2. What does happen to imprisoned criminals, according to the author?
3. Where does the author believe society's protection does lie?

Reprinted from *Instead of Prisons: A Handbook for Abolitionists*, F.H. Knopp, et al., Safer Society Press, 3049 East Genesee St., Syracuse, NY 13224. (315) 446-6151. $12 per copy including shipping costs. Bulk rates available.

Myth: Prisons protect society from "criminals."

Reality: Prisons fail to protect society from "criminals," except for a very small percentage and only temporarily. Prisons "protect" the public only from those few who get caught and convicted, thereby serving the primary function of control over certain segments of society.

According to Norman Carlson, director of the Federal Bureau of Prisons, "The goal of our criminal justice system is to protect law-abiding citizens from crime, particularly crimes of violence, and to make them secure in their lives and property." Despite shifts in "correctional" emphases, restraint or keeping the "criminal" out of circulation continues to be a key purpose of prisons. However, it is questionable how much real protection prisons afford, because only a small percent of all lawbreakers end up in prison and most of these few remain in prison for a relatively short period of time.

Prisons have pacified the public with the image of "safety," symbolized by walls and cages located in remote areas. But prisons are a massive deception: seeming to "protect," they engender hostility and rage among all who are locked into the system, both prisoner and keeper. Society is victimized by the exploitation of its fear of crime.

Indeed, rather than protecting society from the harmful, prisons are in themselves harmful. It is likely that persons who are caged will become locked into a cycle of crime and fear, returning to prison again and again. Prisons are selectively damaging to specific groups in society; namely, Blacks and other minorities.

The Few Who Get Caught

The failure of prisons to protect is bound up with the reality of who actually gets caught. According to the system managers, true protection would require a high degree of effectiveness. The system, however, is highly ineffective. Few lawbreakers are apprehended and most studies show that only one to three percent of all reported crime results in imprisonment. In one study, out of 100 major crimes (felonies): 50 were reported to the police; suspects were arrested in 12 of the cases; six persons were convicted; one or two went to prison.

Those who find themselves entrapped in the criminal (in)justice systems most often are a select group, usually stereotype "criminals"—a threat in some way to those in power: the poor, minorities, the young. Very few of the total lawbreaking population are ever caught, and an estimated one-half to three-fourths of all crime is never reported. How can prison-as-protection be anything but an illusion?

The objection is often raised: "Better to be protected at least from that small minority of lawbreakers who *are* convicted." What, then, is the nature of this protection? According to Milton Rector, president of the National Council on Crime and Delinquency:

People who feel reassured by the high walls of the prison, its sentries, control towers and its remoteness from population centers are naive. Most prisoners leave their institutions at some point. In the United States, 95 percent are released after an average imprisonment of 24 to 32 months. . . . So the protection offered by the prison during the incarceration of the offender is surely a short term insurance policy and a dubious one at that.

Warehousing Is Temporary

We can see then, that if prison protects at all, warehousing is only temporary, for most all prisoners are ultimately released back into society, usually within two to three years. Moreover, the deterrent effect of prisons, on individuals and on the larger society, is highly questionable. There is no insurance of further "protection" from criminal activity beyond release.

ROTHCO

VADILLO - SIEMPRE, MEXICO

5-29E48

© Vadillo/Rothco

One commonly cited occurrence which illustrates the dubious nature of the protection theory followed a U.S. Supreme Court ruling in 1963 known as *Gideon v. Wainwright,* which affirmed the right of indigent felony defendants to counsel. Those convicted without counsel and sent to prison were ordered released. As a result, the State of Florida released 1,252 indigent felons before their sentences were completed. There was fear that such a mass exodus from prison might result in an increase in crime. However, after 28 months, the Florida Department of Corrections found that the recidivism rate for these ex-prisoners was only 13.6 percent, compared to 25 percent for those released after completing their full sentences. An American Bar Association committee commenting on the case observed:

> Baldly stated, . . . if we, today, turned loose all of the inmates of our prisons without regard to the length of their sentences, and

with some exceptions, without regard to their previous offenses, we might reduce the recidivism rate over what it would be if we kept each prisoner incarcerated until his sentence expired.

For more than a century, statisticians have demonstrated that regardless of imprisonment, the crime rate remains constant. Removing some few people from society simply means an unapprehended majority continue in criminal activity. If that one to three percent who end up in prison were released, they would not significantly increase the lawbreaking population.

The Few Society Fears

The myth of protection relies on society's perception of the "criminal" from whom it wishes to be safeguarded. Fear necessitates fortresses. The myth of the criminal type has led to penitentiaries that "are placed out in the country as if they were for lepers or for people with contagious diseases."

There is a critical distinction between who is "caught" and who poses a danger to society. Police act upon a stereotype which accounts for a "very marked relationship between class and conviction." The purpose of police activity is seen "in a manner somewhat analogous to the forceful quarantining of persons with infectious diseases . . . to control and suppress the activity of this lower class criminal subgroup." Thus, those who are caught because feared (by the police) are feared (by the public) because caught. The notion that "crime is the vice of a handful of people" is grossly inaccurate. As William Ryan states in *Blaming the Victim:*

> Crime is extraordinarily prevalent in this country. It is endemic. We are surrounded and immersed in crime. In a very real sense, most of our friends and neighbors are law violators. Large numbers of them are repeated offenders. A very large group have committed serious major felonies, such as theft, assault, tax evasion, and fraud.

Once we accept the idea that most "criminals" are relatively indistinguishable from the rest of the population, it becomes evident that prisons "are full of people needlessly and inappropriately detained and incarcerated." The additional fact that most prisoners have been convicted of property related crimes, not crimes of violence, further calls into question the concept that society needs protection from the vast majority of those who are currently imprisoned.

Prisons are also viewed as a means of protecting society from that small percentage of lawbreakers who commit violent crimes . . . . The concept of labelling persons as "dangerous" assumes an ability to predict future behavior. Which "criminals" are likely to commit future crimes of violence when released? Given a "most remarkable void of reliable analysis," predictions of "dangerousness" cannot be trusted. For instance, a murderer—the typical image of a dangerous criminal—is highly unlikely to murder again.

Most murderers "could be let out tomorrow without endangering the public safety." . . .

A permanent prison banishment of the many convicted and restrained for the sake of safety from a possible few, is not only morally outrageous but economically unfeasible . . . .

Prisons Create Danger

We can predict some of the responses by those who are subjected to the brutalizing environment of prisons. Resentment, rage and hostility on the part of both keeper and kept, are the punitive dividends society reaps as a result of caging. A stunning realization evolves: the punishment of prison damages persons, and consequently, creates *more* danger to society. Furthermore, the coercive institutional environment encourages violence among prisoners themselves. Who "protects" this segment of the citizenry? . . . .

Do They Protect Society?

Nope. Prisons might have some protective benefits if hard-core criminals were locked away in them forever, but as it is, temporary inmates are mixed with permanent ones, nonviolent inmates with violent ones, first-timers with veterans. It would be hard to design a better school for criminals than a U.S. prison. Anti-crime campaigns that rely on locking away more and more criminals are the unwitting supporters of such "schools" and probably make the streets less safe in the long run.

Kenneth Guentert, *U.S. Catholic*, June 1983.

The negative effects of caging reach beyond prison walls, allowing citizens a false sense of safety. Prisons, by their very existence, exonerate communities from the responsibilities of providing the necessary human services which might effectively reduce "crime."

Society's greatest protection can be found in the development of reconciling communities—not in walls and cages. There is very little connection between putting a person in prison and protection of society from the harm of crime. The harm of prisons overwhelms any benefit of protection.

Determining Punishments

The subject of appropriate punishments for crimes committed in society is controversial. Throughout history and in different civilizations the issue of how and of how much to punish provides interesting comparisons. The ancient Code of Hammurabi focused on making the punishment fit the crime, a type of exact justice. A pickpocket would have his hand cut off, for example. This is the same concept as the Old Testament philosophy of an eye for an eye and a tooth for a tooth. These codes of punishment were all attempts to make the wrongdoer suffer as much as the victim of the crime. Another example of crimes and fitting punishments is found in Dante's *Purgatory*, in which the seven deadly sins are skillfully punished through acts that not only match the crime, but also work toward atonement:

The envious: the eyelids were sewn with wire since they had looked with envy on others.

The angry: Their ire is shrouded in a thick dark cloud of smoke.

The greedy and prodigal: They must lay on their stomachs, hands and feet bound. Their souls were once tied to their great greed, now their bodies are tied to the ground.

The fornicators: Purged by the very fire of their passions, they are deposited in flaming holes of fire.

The gluttonous: Kept in an emaciated state, just out of reach of a fresh fruit tree and fresh water.

The arrogant: Because they kept their bodies and souls too erect on earth, they must carry great rocks on their backs which keep their faces bent to the ground.

(Excerpted from *Just and Painful* by Graeme R. Newman.)

While these grotesque and cruel punishments are vastly different than the public system of justice we have in the United States, they raise a number of questions. Do punishments have to make people suffer to be effective? Certainly there is a lively debate in this book as to whether prisons have become too comfortable to be effective, or, the opposite, that they are already inhumane warehouses. Should a civilized society punish in this way? Does a civilized society have an obligation to be humane, and perhaps even try to reintegrate criminals into society? And what about the seemingly hopeless cases—the mass murderers and sociopaths for whom no punishment would be effective? How much should economic and environmental factors in the lives of criminals count in the issue of punishment? Should a child abuser who was an abused child himself be psychologically treated or locked up like any other criminal? Keep these questions in mind when completing the following activity.

Instructions:

Consider the crimes and punishments below. Assign what you believe to be the most appropriate punishment for each crime. If you are doing this activity as a member of a class, work in a small group and attempt to come to a consensus on each punishment before moving on to the next crime. Be able to explain the reasoning behind your sentencing. The punishments listed are meant to be rough guidelines. You may use different punishments or combinations.

punishment	crime
_____	**child abuse** male offender sexually abused a four-year-old girl
_____	**child abuse** male offender, who himself was abused as a child, sexually abused a four-year-old girl
_____	**murder** alcoholic father with a history of depression murdered entire family of four after a drinking binge
_____	**murder** individual murdered 18 people in a MacDonald's restaurant for no apparent reason
_____	**murder** husband murdered wife after discovering wife had been having an affair for several years
_____	**murder** wife murdered husband after being mentally and physically abused by husband for 12 years
_____	**shoplifting** woman stole cosmetics from supermarket
_____	**petty theft** person robbed a grocery store pleading he did not have enough food to feed his family
_____	**theft** white-collar worker embezzled $250,000 from employer

49

_____ **robbery** juvenile robbed a convenience store, third offense

_____ **bank robbery** individual robbed six banks while on parole for a similar offense

_____ **rape** person rapes a woman stranger, first offense

_____ **rape** man has been convicted of three rapes and is suspected of seven. He has been in and out of prison for previous rape convictions

punishments

probation
victim compensation
psychological treatment
community work
1 to 12 months imprisonment
1 to 5 years imprisonment
5 to 10 years imprisonment
10 years or more imprisonment
life imprisonment
death penalty
other (be specific)

Bibliography

The following list of books, periodicals, and pamphlets deals with the subject matter of this chapter.

Frances A. Allen	*The Decline of the Rehabilitative Ideal*, New Haven, CT: Yale University Press, 1981.
Louis B. Cei	"Prison Rehabilitation Programs Do Work," *USA Today*, July 1983.
Francis T. Cullen and Karen E. Gilbert	*Reaffirming Rehabilitation*, Cincinnati, OH: Anderson Publishing Co., 1982.
Kathleen Engel and Stanley Rothman	"The Paradox of Prison Reform: Rehabilitation, Prisoners' Rights, and Violence," *Harvard Journal of Law and Public Policy*, Vol. 7, No. 2, 1984.
Harper's	"Images of Fear," May 1985.
Robert Martinson, Ted Palmer, and Stuart Adams	*Rehabilitation, Recidivism, and Research.* Pamphlet available from National Council on Crime and Delinquency, 2125 Center Avenue, Fort Lee, NJ 07024. 1976.
Gordon Mehler	"Inmates Need Jobs," *The New York Times*, July 17, 1984.
Karl Menninger	*The Crime of Punishment*, New York: Viking Press, 1966.
Thomas O. Murton	*The Dilemma of Prison Reform*, New York: Irvington Publishers, Inc., 1982.
Henry N. Pontell	*A Capacity to Punish*, Bloomington, IN: Indiana University Press, 1984.
Robert Stout	"Going Straight: Without Help, It's Almost Impossible to Make It," *Commonweal*, January 16, 1981.
Stuart Taylor Jr.	"Strict Penalties for Criminals: Pendulum of Feeling Swings," *The New York Times*, December 13, 1983.
U.S. News & World Report	"Bulging Prisons: Curbing Crime or Wasting Lives?" April 23, 1984.
James Q. Wilson	*Crime & Public Policy*, San Francisco: ICS Press, 1983.

How Do Prisons
Affect Criminals?

"No one has ever come out of prison a better man."

Prisons Create a Criminal Personality

Jack Henry Abbott

In prison since his early teens, Jack Henry Abbott has spent his lifetime in jail. With the publication of his book *In the Belly of the Beast*, from which this viewpoint is taken, he became a literary sensation. Norman Mailer, a prominent novelist and biographer, wrote a long and laudatory article for *The New York Times* about Abbott, in which he argued that it was a tragedy that such a talented writer should be wasting away in jail. Mailer continued to campaign for his early release, and in June 1981 his hopes were realized. Abbott's new-found freedom lasted scarcely a month. In July, 1981 Abbott murdered a 22-year-old bartender in a barroom dispute. Although these events cast doubts on the idea of rehabilitating prisoners, Abbott's letters remain a poignant and powerful testimony to life in prison. In the following viewpoint, Mr. Abbott describes how prison's dehumanizing effects actually create a criminal personality, leaving the prisoner's emotional state forever mangled by hate, distrust and fear.

As you read, consider the following questions:

1. What evidence does Mr. Abbott cite so the reader will believe that he does not "belong in prison"?
2. How is rehabilitation practiced in prison, according to the author?

From *In the Belly of the Beast* by Jack Henry Abbott. Copyright © 1981 by Jack Henry Abbott. Reprinted by permission of Random House, Inc.

Can you imagine how I feel—to be treated as a little boy and not as a man? And when I was a little boy, I was treated as a man—and can you imagine what that does to a boy? (I keep waiting for the years to give me a sense of humor, but so far that has evaded me completely.)

So. A guard frowns at me and says: "Why are you not at work?" Or: "Tuck in your shirttail!" Do this and do that. The way a little boy is spoken to. This is something I have had to deal with not for a year or two—nor even ten years—but for, so far, eighteen years. And when I explode, then I have burnt myself by behaving like a contrite and unruly little boy. So I have, in order to avoid that deeper humiliation, developed a method of reversing the whole situation—and I become the man chastising the little boy. (Poor kid!) It has cost me dearly, and not just in terms of years in prison or in the hole.

I cannot adjust to daily life in prison. For almost twenty years this has been true. I have never gone a month in prison without incurring disciplinary action for violating "rules." Not in all these years.

Does this mean I must die in prison? Does this mean I cannot "adjust" to society outside prison?

The government answers *yes*—but I *remember* society, and it is not like prison. I feel that if I ever did *adjust to prison*, I could by that alone never adjust to society. I would be back in prison within months.

Now, I care about myself and I cannot let it happen that I cannot adjust to freedom. Even if it means spending my life in prison—because to me prison is nothing but mutiny and revolt.

. . . A round peg will not fit into a square slot. I don't think they'll ever let me out of prison so long as my release depends upon my "good adjustment to prison."

I Don't Belong in Prison

In the beginning the walls of my cell were made of boiler-plate steel, and I would kick them all day every day, hollering, screaming—for no apparent reason. I was so choked with rage in those days (about sixteen or seventeen years ago), I could hardly talk, even when I was calm: I *stuttered* badly. I used to throw my tray as casually as you would toss a balled-up scrap of paper in a trash can—but would do it with a tray full of food at the face of a guard.

That is what I mean by a response to the prison experience by a man who does not belong there.

Hell, if I never went to prison, who knows what "evil" I would have committed. I'm not at all saying that because I don't *belong* in prison that I should not have been sent there. Theoretically, *no one* should *belong* in prison! I was sent there for punishment—and

I happen to have gotten it. I do not think it is like that with most men who are sent to prison. Everyone hurts in prison, but not like that . . . .

I have never accepted that I did this to myself. I have never been successfully indoctrinated with that belief. That is the only reason I have been in prison this long.

Indoctrination begins the moment someone is arrested. It becomes more thorough every step of the way, from the moment of arrest to incarceration. In prison, it finds its most profound expression.

Every minute for years you are forced to believe that your suffering is a result of your "ill behavior," that it is self-inflicted. You are indoctrinated to blindly accept *anything* done to you. But if a guard knocks me to the floor, only by indoctrination can I be brought to believe I did it to myself. If I am thrown in the prison hole for having violated a prison rule—for having, for example, shown insolence to a pig—I can only believe I brought this upon myself through *indoctrination* . . . .

Responsibility? I am not responsible for what the government— its system of justice, its prison—has done to me. I did not do this to myself.

That is not easy to say; it is not a *point of view* to hold. Why? Because it has cost me, so far, almost two decades of imprisonment. This I hold is the *greater* responsibility: I did not do this to myself.

Michael Keefe for the Denver Post, reprinted with permission.

I do not share in the sins of this guilty country; we are not "all in this together"! Who in America today would *dare* take the responsibility for himself and others that I and countless other prisoners like me have taken?...

Cowards Are the Norm

. . . The law has never punished anyone for hurting me. If I want justice to punish a wrong done me, it is entirely up to me.

Just picture yourself in that position right there in New York. You can't call a cop or the law when your house is burgled, when you are mugged downtown. The police walk into your home, slap you around (to put it mildly) and help themselves to whatever they want. Your wife and kids even. Anyone there in New York can accuse you of anything and you are punished without even knowing who your accuser is. You have absolutely no rights to legal protection by prosecution. The most you can do is file a civil complaint against the city. Hands are "slapped," but nothing is done. The "slapping of hands" is merely this. The judge says: "Now, Mayor (Warden), I hope this doesn't happen again." That's it. The mayor doesn't even bother to respond to the "admonition." He stands up, stretches, yawns and ambles away. All the faces around you, even the judge's, are covered with smirks. That's it. That's how I have had to live all my life.

What would you do? I assure you, you'd become a deranged coward or the exact opposite. If you become the former, everyone is happy and they'll give you little rewards. If you become the latter, they'll destroy you at every opportunity they get. They'll say you are "crazy," a psycho, etc. The "norm" is the coward in this situation.

Prison and Rehabilitation

To become *rehabilitated* means to accept and live by the values of your society. It requires not just faith in the laws and customs of your society, but faith in the people of your society—and to *extend* those values, and *reproduce* that faith, in your transactions with others in social intercourse.

To rehabilitate someone is a process of teaching. It is a process of *learning* by experience for the man in need of rehabilitation. He requires to know the benefits of the values of his society; he requires a firm understanding of the proper uses of the laws and customs of his society.

Only a man who is a social anomaly can fail to pursue his best interest, especially when the pathway becomes clear to him, for a social anomaly *knows* the values of his society and its laws and customs.

The system of justice in America teaches these lessons to men as if they were social anomalies *already*—as if they had *knowledge* of the values and customs and laws of this society. This reflects the

American maxim: *Ignorance does not acquit.*

So rehabilitation is presumed and American justice seeks to *punish* men who *(theoretically)* know better.

And what does *punishment* that aims at *rehabilitation* entail? It does not aim at winning men over by reason—it is *presumed* a prisoner cannot be won over by reason. It is the application of force.

. . . A system of justice that does not instruct by *reason*, that does not rationally demonstrate to a man the error of his ways, accomplishes the opposite ends of justice: oppression.

No one in any prison in this country has ever been shown the errors of his ways by the law. It is an annoyance no one involved in the administration of justice wants to be bothered with.

So it is relegated to the prison regimes.

Who Belongs in Prison?

Everyone in prison has committed crimes, could be called a criminal. But that does not mean everyone in prison *belongs* there. I would like to suggest that there are men who are justly in prison but do not belong there. And there are men justly in prison who *do belong* there. Perhaps the great majority of prisoners belong there. They keep returning. I've seen at least one entire prison turn over in population. Almost every one of them (in fact, *everyone* I've seen) feels relieved to be back. They need shaves and showers; they are gaunt, starved-looking when they come in from outside. *Within a week* they are rosy-cheeked, starched-and-pressed, talking to everyone. Laughing a lot (hail-fellow-well-met). They fit in in prison.

Prison's Psychological Effects

Naturally it's debatable, but the psychological effects that an institution can have on an individual over a period of years, especially a prison or some other correctional institution, is or can be devastating without the individual even being aware of it . . . .

While in confinement, all responsibility is taken away . . . . Programmed into the system's way of thinking, and in time, many become dependent upon that system and in all reality, lose their identity with society.

James H. Dunn, *The Angolite*, July/August 1983.

This is where they belong. Or, to be more charitable—because if men pursue their best interests, no one really "belongs" in prison—let me say that there are less uncertainties in life in a prison than on the outside. It is not a matter so simple as that they have become institutionalized out of *habit*. That is not it. Prison is much more than a habit with men who belong here.

The point is: there are those—and they are not many, but they

are men for whom prison does punish and punishes every day—
who do not belong here in prison . . . .

Society to Blame

Society and not prison prevents their rehabilitation. For rehabilitation is something we *all* stand in need of; the rehabilitation of
society itself has not been accomplished. This is reflected *also* in
the fact that so many men in prison are not rehabilitated there
(there in prison).

If society is so intolerable that a man can only feel himself to be
a man in prison, it is the "fault" of society.

And I suggest that a few men are constantly rehabilitated in
prison: they belong in society or they belong to the dead. But not
in prison.

. . . No one has ever come out of prison a better man. I'm not talking about places like Allenwood and Maxwell Field—the places
they send government informers and that frail species of individual
who falls from the graces of the government or the Republican
party or the Stock Exchange.

I'm speaking of the *penitentiary*. There is at least one in every
state. Some states—like New York, Texas, California, Michigan,
Illinois—have at least a half-dozen of them. The federal government
itself has over forty prisons but only about a half-dozen
penitentiaries . . . .

Prisoners More Capable of Crime

For almost twenty years I have seen prisoners come and go.
There is not *one* of them who comes to prison for the first time who
is *capable* of the vast repertoire of crimes he is capable of when he
finally gets out of prison. I'm not talking about the fine techni-
calities of, say, safe-cracking or the mechanics of murder. I'm not
talking about methodologies.

No one learns those things in prison, contrary to the government's claims: prisoners do not learn how to commit crimes from
other prisoners . . . .

What is forced down their throats in spite of themselves is *the will*
to commit crimes. It is the *capability* I am speaking of.

It used to be a pastime of mine to watch the change in men, to
observe the blackening of their hearts. It takes place before your
eyes. They enter prison more bewildered than afraid. Every step
after that, the fear creeps into them. They are experiencing men
and the administration of things no novels or the cinema—nor even
the worst rumors about prison—can teach. No one is prepared for
it. Even the pigs, when they first start to work in prison, are not
prepared for it.

Everyone is afraid. It is not an emotional, psychological fear. It is
a practical matter. If you do not threaten someone—at the very
least—someone will threaten you. When you walk across the yard

or down the tier to your cell, you stand out like a sore thumb if you do not appear either callously unconcerned or cold and ready to kill.

Many times you have to "prey" on someone, or you will be "preyed" on yourself. After so many years, *you are not bluffing*. No one is.

Life So Dangerous

For want of a better expression, this is a *cynical experience* of life so *dangerous*, it changes you so that you don't even notice the change in yourself. In five or ten years, it's a way of life. You see pigs commit murder, and everyone from the warden on down are *active* accomplices. That is putting it mildly. The most well-known politicians and judges *actively* suppress evidence of such crimes. They are *rife*. You see it so often, it is routine....

The Crime of Prisons

Prisons subject inmates to violence, extortion, and rape. That is crime—not punishment. As long as prisons are like that (and everyone agrees that a great many are), then those prisons themselves are crimes. And those who advocate sending human beings to them apply God's law selectively.

John F. Alexander, *The Other Side*, October 1982.

By the time you get out—*if* you get out—you are capable of *anything*, any crime at all.

Have you ever seen a man *despair* because he cannot bring himself to murder? I am not talking about murder in the heat of combat—that very seldom occurs in prison—I am speaking of cold-blooded premeditated murder. The only prisoners I have ever seen who do not suffer from that despair of being incapable of murder are those who *are* capable of it (not a few).

The Capability to Murder

Most of them find—somewhere down the line—that they *are* capable of it. To discover that there was no basis for your anxieties about murder is a feeling similar to that of a young man who has doubts about being capable of consummating his first sexual encounter with a woman—and when the time comes, if he did not perform magnificently, at least he got the job done. You feel stronger.

If you can kill like that, you can do anything. All of the elements of every crime come into play. There is the deception; the ability to hold a secret; the calculation; the nerve—and the activity of well-planned and executed *violence*.

Most important, you learn never to trust a man, even if he seems

59

honest and sincere. You learn how men deceive themselves and how impossible it is to help them without injuring yourself.

You know all of this and more in a conscious way before you get out of prison.

Why do you *steal* when you get out? Why do you commit crimes you never dreamed of being able to commit before you entered prison? You have changed so that you are not even aware there was a time you were incapable of such things. If you meditate on it, you tell yourself that you steal because you are no longer afraid of going to prison. This is because you do not remember you were not afraid originally.

*"One major [criticism] that is inaccurate and
misleading is branding correctional institutions
as schools for crime."*

The Criminal Personality
Exists Before Prison

Stanton E. Samenow

Stanton E. Samenow, a clinical psychologist, is in private practice
in Alexandria, Virginia. He is a consultant and speaker on criminal
behavior and a member of President Reagan's Task Force on
Victims of Crime. During his eight years as research psychologist
at Saint Elizabeth's Hospital in Washington, DC, he co-authored,
with the late Dr. Samuel Yochelson, the much-heralded three-
volume study *The Criminal Personality*. In the following viewpoint,
Mr. Samenow states that it is not prison that is the corrupting influence in the lives of criminals, but the opposite: criminals corrupt
the prison system. A criminal's personality does not stop being
criminal in prison. He or she just continues to exhibit the same
mind-set once in prison.

As you read, consider the following questions:

1. Does Mr. Samenow believe that criminals are imprisoned
   unjustly? Why or why not?
2. How does a criminal employ "psychological warfare,"
   according to Mr. Samenow?
3. Does the author believe that criminals can "outgrow" crime?
   Why or why not?

From *Inside the Criminal Mind* by Stanton E. Samenow. Copyright © 1984 by Stanton E.
Samenow. Reprinted by permission of Times Books, a division of Random House, Inc.

In mid-1982, there were 394,380 inmates in prison in the United States. Over the last two decades, the prison reform movement has gathered strength, and much of the criticism leveled at correctional facilities has been constructive. However, one major thrust that is inaccurate and misleading is branding correctional institutions as schools for crime with the implication that people are turned into something that they weren't before.

Prison is a breeding ground for crime only insofar as a criminal expands his associations and finds support for antisocial patterns of thought and behavior. He hears new ideas for crime in prison, but *he* is the one who accepts or rejects those ideas. No one forces him to continue a life of crime either within the institution or when he returns to society. He is not a hapless victim who is corrupted by fellow inmates. He has made choices in the past and continues to make choices.

Criminals Remain the Same

Criminals exhibit the same behavior patterns inside prison as on the streets. Being locked up does not alter a criminal's perception that he is top dog. Once he adjusts to his surroundings, he becomes determined to establish himself, his stance being, "If you serve time, let time serve you." And so he continues his manipulations and power plays. Some inmates abide by the rules, but not because of any inner personality transformation. Rather, they are building themselves up as model inmates in order to gain special status or privileges. Then there are the inmates who find incarceration to be truly unsettling, if not a major crisis in their lives. They make genuine efforts to change, even seeking the help of institutional counselors, but the counseling that they receive usually turns out to be inadequate.

Wherever he is sent, the criminal believes that confinement is the final injustice in a string of injustices that began with his arrest. In the past, laws and others' rights meant little to him, but now that he is confined, he becomes highly legalistic about asserting his own rights. One inmate who was serving a sentence for a string of burglaries acknowledged, "You break a law to get what you want and treasure the law when it gets you what you want." The criminal looks for a way to beat a charge, and even long after he has begun serving his sentence, he seeks a means to overturn a verdict or reduce his sentence. Some spend hours poring over law books in the prison library and weeks laboring over writs. Among them are men who make a career in prison as jailhouse lawyers, conducting legal research and preparing documents for themselves and other inmates, collecting, in the latter case, money, property, and personal favors. . . .

Despite being behind bars, the criminal still expects to do as he pleases. This is not surprising because it is a lifelong attitude.

However, inmates have different methods of getting what they want in prison just as they did outside. Some wage open warfare with staff members, flouting authority and brazenly defying regulations. One teenager bragged about his defiance in a state institution: "I tore up my room. I loved hearing glass break." At another juvenile facility, several ringleaders assembled all the kids of one unit, barricaded the staff out of the lounge, and demolished the place. Some prisoners prefer to be locked in their cells or banished to "the hole" rather than capitulate to anyone. Even in their cells they can create a commotion by setting bedding afire or cause floods by stuffing up toilets. Said one inmate, "I am going to play my cards the way I want to and when I want to. Go straight—hell! I would rather remain a hoodlum than let anyone walk over me. No one is going to stop me unless they kill me."

The Criminal's Contempt for Society

Unless criminals are serving terms of life without parole, which very few do, they will be free eventually to prey upon us all. There is still a job for corrections to do in the institution and the community— that is to correct. But rehabilitation as it has been practiced cannot possibly be effective because it is based on a total misconception. To rehabilitate is to restore to a former constructive capacity or condition. *There is nothing to which to rehabilitate a criminal.* There is no earlier condition of being responsible to which to restore him. He never learned the ways of getting along in this world that most of us learned as children. Just as rehabilitation is a misconception, so too is the notion of "reintegrating the criminal into the community." It is absurd to speak of reintegrating him when he was never integrated in the first place. The criminal has long stood apart from the community, contemptuous of people who lived responsibly.

Stanton E. Samenow, *Inside the Criminal Mind*, 1984.

In a struggle for status among fellow cons, the physically aggressive inmate is quick to lash out with a stream of profanity or throw a punch whenever he feels infringed upon. A prisoner who calls him a string of names may wind up with a fork jammed in his gut. A melee may erupt when someone switches the channel on the television. An unaware staff member may suffer a fractured skull from a flying chair after denying an inmate's request. One irascible inmate, displeased with the vegetable soup served at lunch, stared into his bowl, glowered at the man serving him, and complained that he had received the "dregs of the pot." He declared the "slop" unfit to eat and demanded another portion. When the worker ignored him, he threw the soup in his face. . . .

Whether he locks horns with the staff or cons his way into their good graces, the criminal wages psychological warfare. With his customary finesse, he preys upon human insecurity, weakness, greed, and prejudice. Knowing how staff members feel about him and other inmates may be of considerable advantage. If he can touch a sensitive nerve, he may provoke a staff member into losing control. It is a triumph to divert attention from himself and put the other person or even the whole institution on the defensive. . . .

Don't Snitch

In prison, just as on the street, the dilemma of whom to trust hangs heavily in the air. Criminals don't know what trust is. If they use the word, it usually means that a person won't betray them. "Don't snitch" is a code among inmates. The price of squealing on another con may be a beating or even death. Even so, the inmate realizes that every man is out for himself and that even his best buddy may turn informant to save his own skin or to acquire privileges. Although convicts share an understanding of "no snitching," the dominant ethos in prison is, as it was outside, "[Damn] everybody else but me." Writing in *Corrections Magazine*, Stephen Gettinger reports, "Some prison observers say that the inmate code's prohibitions against informing are more honored in the breach than in the observance. The trading of information is as common, and as necessary, to the daily life of any prison as taking the count." . . .

A criminal's absorption with crime does not necessarily diminish just because he is locked up. Despite the restrictive environment, he schemes, talks about, and continues to engage in illicit activities. Any external stimulus, such as a television cop show, a detective movie, or a lurid crime story in the paper feeds an already busy mind, as do his daily conversations with other inmates about crime. Through letters and visitors, the criminal hangs on to old ties in addition to establishing new ones in prison. To some, confinement means that the challenge to engage in illicit activities is greater than ever. Theft is rampant in prisons. Anything that a man wants to hold on to must be kept on his person or surrendered to a trustworthy staff member. An inmate may be robbed when he sleeps (if he shares a cell or dormitory), while he takes a shower, or at any other moment when he relaxes his guard. Inmates not only steal from one another but also pilfer personal belongings from the staff and food and other supplies from the institution. . . .

Criminals Are Criminals

All the above is intended to underscore the point that criminals are criminals, no matter where they are. In prison, their personality remains as it was. What may vary is the degree of risk they will take and therefore the method by which they operate. Those abstaining from crime still miss it, but they content themselves with fantasy and conversation about crime. Said a 22-year-old burglar, "I'm still not afraid while I sit here in prison. The only thing I think

©Beutel/Rothco

about is stealing when I'm out of here in a few years and not the consequences. They don't mean anything.''

No criminal wants to return to prison, and no criminal expects to. Some offenders serve time, and that in itself is a powerful deterrent to further criminal activity. They do not repeat. But these are not the people who have made crime a way of life. There are no studies of these people and no figures as to how numerous they are.

Contrary to what some people believe, most criminals do learn from experience, but it is not what society wants to teach him. In prison, such a person has ample time and opportunity to learn how to be a better criminal. Some decide that upon release they will lie low, limit themselves to smaller crimes, and forgo the big-time ventures. Or perhaps they will mastermind a crime but stay behind the scenes rather than participate directly in the action. Such intentions are short-lived. Once they leave prison behind, their appetites become voracious for the high excitement of the old life. Some in fact do become more successful criminals, immersing themselves heavily in crime but being slick enough to avoid apprehension. Others avoid arrest for a long time but eventually land back in the slammer. Then there are the big losers. Hardly has the prison disgorged them into society than they slip up, get caught, and are charged with a new offense.

Can Never Outgrow Crime

It is widely believed that criminals outgrow crime, but this is based on the fact that some never return to prison. Rand Corporation researchers observe that some criminologists have hypothesized that the criminal reaches a "burnout stage." Dr. Richard Schwartz states, "By the time a man reaches age 40 his criminal career is essentially over." The burnout theory may be based on the fact that some older criminals cease to get arrested for street crimes. It is true that as the street criminal ages, he is not as agile and literally cannot run as fast as he used to. He has mellowed only in that he takes fewer big risks and his offenses may be less serious. But his criminal personality remains unchanged, and people still suffer at his hands.

"Prison violence is being exacerbated not only by the unprecedented growth of the prison population. . . but by the kinds of facilities in which we house our criminal population."

Prisons Are Violent and Dehumanizing

Steve Lerner

A long-standing argument against the use of prisons is that they represent cruel and unusual punishment. Antiquated prisons are still in use, making prison conditons intolerably overcrowded and unsanitary. Steve Lerner, a freelance writer based in New York, declares in the following viewpoint that these conditions need to be rectified by building safer, more comfortable prisons.

As you read, consider the following questions:

1. What is the most dangerous aspect of prisons, according to the author?
2. Why does the author believe that the reader should be concerned about prison violence?
3. How does the author believe that the public can encourage the building of safe jails?

Steve Lerner, "Rule of the Cruel," *The New Republic*, October 15, 1984. Reprinted by permission of *The New Republic*, © 1984, The New Republic, Inc.

Contrary to what most of us assume from stories in the press, it is not riots and the taking of hostages that is the most prevalent and dangerous form of violence in prison but attacks upon inmates by other inmates. Although there is a dearth of hard statistics, there is no question that noncollective violence has been escalating in our prisons since the 1960s. I recently toured seven adult jails and prisons for men in New York and spent two years studying correctional facilities for California's most violent young offenders. The dozens of inmates, correctional officers, criminologists, prison administrators, architects, and planners whom I interviewed agreed that prison violence is being exacerbated not only by the unprecedented growth of the prison population in the past decade, but by the kinds of facilities in which we house our criminal population....

Although approaches to working with prisoners change from decade to decade, prison architecture is less flexible. Once a mistaken design is adopted, the facility can last for up to a hundred years. For example, at least half of all felons are currently incarcerated in maximum-security facilities built more than seventy years ago, even though many of these institutions have long been judged obsolete or inappropriate. Thus the way in which we spend the billions of dollars appropriated for construction will lock us into a criminal justice strategy for the next century. Our current tactic of cloning prisons that have proved over the decades to be inhuman, inefficient, costly, and dangerous is a mistake of enormous magnitude....

Countless Violent Outbursts

There are countless sources of conflict in crowded and ill-designed prisons like Attica and Sing Sing, which are structured and administered in a way that ensures the safety of neither prisoners nor guards. Race riots can break out over whether the TV is tuned to an English- or a Spanish-speaking station. Melees have been sparked by disputes over how long someone is spending on the only available public telephone. Bad food, cold food, or food that isn't served on time can cause a prison to erupt. The drug traffic, protection rackets, sex, and arguments over poker debts can also incite bloody violence....

It is impossible to know how many inmates are killed or hurt through prison violence. The number of deaths attributed to "unknown causes" or "accidents" makes the total number of inmates murdered nebulous, but a good guess would be that many of these inmates were killed by unidentified assailants. According to Lawrence Greenfeld, a statistician at the Justice Department's Bureau of Justice Statistics, of the 779 inmates of state and federal prisons reported to have died in 1982 (the statistics do not include those who died in local jails) 357 died of non-natural causes. Of these deaths, 99 were "caused by another," 147 were from

68

"unknown causes," 92 were suicides, and 19 were "accidents."
Greenfeld points out that the murder rate of inmates is actually
lower than it is among men of the same age not in prison. However,
when one adds the number of inmates who died from "unknown
causes" to those whose deaths were "caused by another," the rate
of violent death in prison exceeds that in the outside world.

Inmates and Guards

In addition to inmate-against-inmate violence, there is always the
potential of violence between inmates and guards. Although most
inmates are probably more afraid of one another than they are of
the guards, some inmates fear guard brutality the most. "There's
a war going on here," says Jack Archie, a young, bespectacled black
man from Buffalo who is serving a four-and-a-half to nine-year term
at Attica. Archie complains that the guards don't "show the inmates
any respect." There is talk, he adds, that inmates are beaten by
guards as they are being taken to the Segregated Housing Unit—
the disciplinary lock-up area—for infractions of the rules.

Marked by Brutalization

There is in addition a need to emphasize that a person sent to a penal
facility for a long period will one day be returned to society, not as
a tabula rasa but marked in negative ways by all he or she has experienced in the brutalizing atmosphere of prison life. A chaplain at
Rikers Island summed up the significance of the marks in this way:
"If you put a violent person in prison for a number of years, he'll
come out more violent than before, more liable to inflict physical
harm on others." It is to be hoped that Americans may eventually
perceive that imprisoning fewer, for shorter periods, could result in
an increase rather than a decrease in the personal safety of citizens
everywhere.

George M. Anderson, *America*, May 8, 1982.

I was denied permission to visit the Segregated Housing Unit at
both Attica and Sing Sing. According to prison administrators, the
unit is no different from other parts of the prison except that certain privileges extended elsewhere in the prison are suspended.
Officials also explain that a number of the disciplinary cells are
covered with plexiglass so that inmates cannot throw cups of urine
or exrement at passing guards. Inmates in Segregated Housing are
grounded in the cell twenty-three hours a day. They are not allowed
out to fraternize with other prisoners in the big recreation yard, in
the communal cafeterias, or at work assignments. At the canteen
they are allowed only to buy hygienic products and stationery.
Finally, they can have neither a radio nor a tape recorder to pass
the time. The law requires, however, that they be allowed out of

their cells an hour a day for exercise, that they have access to books from the law library, and that they be allowed visits from friends and relatives. . . .

Why Should You Care?

Why should you care about prison violence? There are a couple of good selfish reasons. The most obvious is that you or someone close to you may one day find yourself in jail on some petty charge and end up being savaged. More compelling is the argument that prison has become one of the chief brutalizing agents in our society, making life less safe for all of us. It doesn't take a multi-million dollar study or a Ph.D. to recognize that men and women who have been subjected to brutality in our prisons are likely to pass on their trauma once released. And don't think they won't be released: more than nine out of ten of those we incarcerate end up back on the streets. When a man—humiliated by the conditions of his confinement and outraged by his treatment at the hands of inmates and guards—subsequently takes out his rage on the first defenseless civilian who has the misfortune of crossing his path, the cycle of violence is complete.

This does not mean that we should abandon the use of prisons, as some advocate. Rather, it suggests that we should build better, safer prisons and be considerably more selective about whom we put in them. Our current strategy of locking up growing numbers of people for longer terms in more and more crowded facilities is producing prison graduates who are increasingly violent. This is hardly a service to society. . . .

No Solution to Crime

Second, there is a lack of strong political leadership willing to confront the popular myth that locking up more people constitutes a solution to crime. Though there are certain violent criminals who must be locked up and kept off the street, there is a much larger number of less serious offenders for whom prison is a costly and inefficient response. What is now lacking is the political will to back the development of alternatives to jail and to support the judges who prescribe them for these less serious cases. . . .

The renovated Manhattan House of Detention in New York City, known for years as the Tombs, is an example of the "new generation jail." Judge Morris Lasker, who in the early 1970s described the old Tombs as the American equivalent of the Black Hole of Calcutta, closed the jail in 1974. Before it was condemned, some 2,000 inmates were routinely held in the facility which had been designed for 800. The Tombs re-opened in October 1983; it now has a capacity of only 421. In addition to this substantial reduction in population, the renovated jail provides each inmate with his own room and a window that looks out on the city. Tension among inmates is further reduced by dividing the institution's population

"If they were smart they wouldn't do a thing about overcrowding. This is a real deterrent to crime!"

© Pearson/Rothco

into three manageable mini-jails, each with its own supervisory staff. These mini-jails are further divided into living units of thirty-eight cells which are clustered in a semicircle around a day room. A correctional officer sitting at a control station can see the entrance of all the rooms and let inmates in or out of them with the flip of a switch.

Inmates Allowed to Visit Others

The outstanding feature of this new concept in jail design is that by clustering small groups of cells around common rooms and allowing inmates to go in and out of their rooms pretty much as they like during the day, the inmates gain control over their dealings with others. This in turn allows them to relax and be less aggressive in protecting their territory. Furthermore, whereas the old-style jail cells are built in a long line that lets out onto a corridor, here they open onto a common room where inmates and correctional officers rub shoulders. This is crucial because it means that the guards no longer cede control of communal living areas to the strongest inmates, as frequently happens in old-fashioned facilities. . . .

Making Jails Safe

How good should a jail be? How safe is safe enough? For my money, a good jail should be safe enough for an innocent man or woman to stay there without being unduly jeopardized. If prisons have a dense population of violent people, they also have a high density of law enforcement supervision. Perhaps one way to encourage the development of safe jails would be to require lawyers and judges to spend two weeks in jail every five years. This would put a powerful lobby behind improving prison conditions. Something on this order happened in Nevada in 1971, when twenty-three judges spent a single night in Nevada State Prison. They emerged from the prison, *Time* magazine reports, appalled at the homosexuality and inmate bitterness, and at men "raving, screaming, and pounding the walls." Judge E. Newton Vickers said "I felt like an animal in a cage" and recommended that bulldozers be dispatched to tear the "damn thing to the ground."

Realistically, of course, we can't tear down all our obsolete prisons—although the worst of them should be replaced as soon as possible. What we certainly can do is make it as safe to be in prison as to be out of it. Prisoners are at once the most despised group in our society and the group most dependent on the protection of the state. Permitting them to serve their punishment in an atmosphere at least as free from terror and violence as the outside world is a test of our collective self-respect, and ultimately a matter of our collective self-interest.

> *"Going to prison should be like reaching a point of no return, like descending into Hell."*

Prison Should Be Dehumanizing

Graeme R. Newman

Graeme R. Newman has written extensively on crime and justice. His book, *The Punishment Response*, is considered the definitive history of punishment. He teaches criminology at the State University of New York, Albany, where he is dean of the School of Criminal Justice. His latest book, *Just and Painful*, from which this viewpoint is excerpted, is a straight-forward case for the use of corporal punishments such as electric shock and whipping. In the following viewpoint, Mr. Newman outlines what he believes prisons should be like: hellish work houses in which criminals are taught the meaning of suffering.

As you read, consider the following questions:

1. What is the essential difference between those who commit crimes and those who don't, according to the author?
2. Under what conditions does the author believe that the pain and suffering of prison is justified?
3. What do you think of Mr. Newman's prison idea? Do you feel it would be justified for the types of criminals Mr. Newman believes should be incarcerated?

Reprinted with permission of The Free Press, a Division of Macmillan, Inc. from *Just and Painful: The Case for the Corporal Punishment of Criminals* by Graeme R. Newman. Copyright © 1983 by Graeme R. Newman.

Acute corporal punishments are more justifiable than prison because they can be limited in their effects more easily to the offender, often only to his actions, leaving the offender's life generally untouched. Prison takes over the whole of the person's life, so that we must justify it only on the basis that the offender either (1) has committed a crime of such proportions that only a punishment that punishes the whole of the offender's life is adequate to fit the crime, or (2) the offender has committed so many crimes that we are justified in punishing him as a criminal rather than for his particular crimes.

In actual fact, both these justifications boil down to the same thing: we are saying that either because of the horror of his single criminal act or because of the terrible extent of his past record, the offender may be viewed as a person imbued with the aura of criminality—in other words that he is an evil person. Thus, it is only through a punishment of similar aura that we can hope to match him or his deeds.

There are red herrings that are thrown across the path of this argument by many social scientists. They claim that researchers have been unable to find any consistent differences between offenders (of any kind of crime) and non-offenders. The reply is:

1. The scientific evidence is inconclusive. Some studies find differences, others do not.

2. Their claims are, frankly, nonsensical, for they ignore the most obvious fact that those offenders they compare us with have in fact committed serious violent crimes, usually a lot of them, and it is this fact that sets them apart from the rest of us. While this point might be more difficult to defend if we were dealing with the whole range of crimes from least to most serious, since probably everyone has committed a little crime or two in the past, it certainly does not apply to the extreme end of the scale which is what we are concerned with in this chapter.

Morality Is the Difference

Very few of those reading this would have committed murder, rape or serious assault or burglary. It is this fact that sets us apart from the criminals who deserve prison. We have little difficulty in judging such criminals as bad persons.

In sum, the difference, the essential difference, between those who have committed a lot of crimes, or just one very serious crime, and the rest of us is one of morality. The modern social scientists, because of their *amorality* have failed to attend to this difference—in fact they try to explain it away.

[I] suggest that only prison terms of 15 years or more should be allowed. While there are good retributive reasons for such a policy, . . . there is another important reason: the goal is to make the gap between us and the truly horrible criminals even greater in

74

practice than before. This is the opposite to the social scientists who keep trying to fudge over the line.

Indeed, going to prison should be like reaching a point of no return, like descending into Hell.

Making Prisons Retributive

To understand the true functions of prison, we must understand that, in contrast to acute corporal punishments, prisons work on a person's mind as well as his body. This fits in with a special kind of retribution which may be called religious retribution, and which takes a basic principle of retribution—that only the guilty should be punished—far more seriously than the old retributivists did.... They were more concerned with rule-breaking than with guilt. In fact it would be more accurate to describe the old retributivists as *secural* retributivists.

The religious retributivists naturally take the word "guilt" in its moral sense, which is to say that the offender has a guilty mind, and that only by a series of ritually purgative functions can this guilt be assuaged. Therefore, one must not only fit the punishment to the crime, but one must fit the punishment to the criminal's guilty mind, and the first step in the process is that the criminal must be contrite, or at least work towards contrition.

Criminals Must Recognize Guilt

The individual must be contrite: he must recognize the error of his ways. He must come to want to make amends, and the only way to effect such a transformation since the sins of evil people are so deeply entrenched, is through a long process of suffering. The originators of American prisons, the Quakers, almost understood this when they thought that solitary confinement and the Bible would be enough. But our prisons have long ago lost contact with their religious roots.

Graeme R. Newman, *Just and Painful*, 1983.

Thus, in answer to those murderers who hypocritically say that "they can't bring back murder victims, so what else can they do?" we say to them: they should suffer the long journey towards contrition. They should work off their guilt, and for some not even a lifetime will be long enough. Surely this is not too much to ask when one considers the innocent lives that they have ruined?

Unfortunately, penologists have lost sight of this important function of retribution, so that they have allowed punishments to destroy souls rather than save them.

One often hears prisons described as soul-destroying. The experience has been likened to Dante's Hell, and aptly so, for the famous inscription above the gates of Dante's Hell is often found scratched on prison walls:

ABANDON HOPE ALL YE WHO ENTER HERE . . .

Prison as Religious Retribution

In Purgatory, Dante, and the Christian religion generally, did not abandon hope, and looked toward the possibility of some kind of salvation, or today we would say cure: salvation is a better word though, since it does not side-step the process of contrition that is inherent in the logic of resolving a crime through its punishment. This is the *religious* as against the *secular* version of retribution.

It is the religious version of retribution that we must apply to the criminals we have locked up, because it is only they whom we have seen fit to imbue with the aura of evil. For those receiving acute corporal punishment and other alternatives, we do not make the leap of judgment to say they are truly evil because they have committed a crime or two of middling seriousness. We punish only their acts, we do not judge their persons. We do not want a Draconian system of criminal justice, and so we save our harshest judgments for only the very few.

Making moral judgments about the quality of the lives of people is an arrogant undertaking, one that should not be taken too lightly, or too often. But once we have made the judgment, we must have the courage to follow up our convictions.

The religious version of retribution requires basically two things: the crime must be resolved through its punishment, and the punishment must involve long term suffering.

The Judeo-Christian tradition has long recognized the importance of ritual suffering as a way of resolving or assuaging the terrible guilt that must fall upon someone who has committed a crime or crimes of unspeakable horror. Most religions do in fact have some equivalent system for dealing with guilt. The pagan religions of classical Greece and Rome were clear about this. The bloody cycle of retributive vengeance in the plays of Aeschylus (*The Orestian Trilogy*) could only be stopped by Orestes spending a long period of time suffering in an effort to assuage the guilt of having murdered his mother. The theme is deeply embedded in western thought.

It is the only way that the cycle of vengeance can be stopped. It is the reason why the trappings of justice—the courts, procedures, dress, etc., have a ritual aura about them . . . .

Treatment in Wolf's Clothing?

The process just described begins to sound very much like a form of "treatment" and not punishment, if one translates it into modern day terminology. For example, instead of talking about the deeper or inner layers of sin that must be penetrated and brought out into the open, one would today talk about uncovering the unconscious, analyzing the offender's inner motives and conflicts.

If this is so, we are in trouble, because criminologists will tell us that it has been found time and time again that treatment does not work, that all manner of treatment programs have been tried out with offenders and none have been shown to produce results any better than chance. That is, criminals who were treated by some method or another who were released, were reconvicted of a subsequent crime in just about the same proportions as those who were released but were not treated.

"The Old Prison Discipline"

Custodial, punitive, and productive practices, sometimes called the "old prison discipline," have been outlined by Howard B. Gill. According to Gill, prison discipline stood for the following:

Hard Labor—Ranging from "making little ones out of big ones" and carrying cannon shot from one end of the prison yard to the other, to constructive prison industries.

Deprivation—Of everything except the requisites for a spartan existence and religious instruction.

Monotony—Essentially no variation in diet and daily routine.

Uniformity—Rigidly consistent treatment of prisoners.

Mass Movement—Individuality was squashed through mass living in cell blocks, mass eating, mass recreation, even mass bathing.

Degradation—To complete the loss of identity, prisoners were housed in monkey cages, dressed in shabby, nondescript clothing, and denied courteous contact with guards.

Subservience—To rules, rules, rules!

Corporal Punishment—Among the uses of force were the paddle, the whip, the sweat box, and the famous boot.

Noncommunication—Absolute silence or solitary confinement, without relief from letters, visits, or other contacts.

Recreation—At first none; later a daily hour in the yard.

No Responsibility—Prisoners were denied every social, civic, domestic, economic, and even personal responsibility.

Isolation—Often 16 hours a day, thereby increasing prisoners' egocentricity.

No "Fraternization" with the Guards—This rule prevented any attempts to solve problems through staff-inmate contacts.

Howard B. Gill, "A New Prison Discipline: Implementing the Declaration of Principles of 1870," *Federal Probation*, Vol. 34, No. 2, June 1970.

But the difference between punishment as cure and the treatment model of penology is substantial. When one reads the punishments described by Dante for those in Purgatory, there is little doubt that they *are* punishments, designed primarily to teach a lesson in a painful way; to ensure that the offender suffers while he learns, through his punishment, the quality of his crime. The religious—and logical—assumption is that a crime is by definition a hurt (whether to others or to oneself), so it is only through hurt that any understanding of one's crime can be reached. In contrast, treatment does not require that the offender suffer any pain at all.

In sum, the proper punishment for a despicable criminal is one that allows for expiation, for a slow learning through a punishment that expresses his crime. It is essential that the basic sin or sins underlying the crime be played out through its opposite so that the individual will learn the evil of his way. For the terrible few, this can only be done through a process of pain and suffering. This is obviously a long and time consuming process, and it is why prison is a most appropriate medium for contrition . . . .

And although, strictly speaking, according to the old retributivists, one should only match the single crime with the single punishment, it is clear from the religious view of retribution that one must match the despicable criminal's *sins* with the punishments, not his *crimes* with the punishments. In other words, one must go beyond the particular offense to the soul of the offender. By this model, one is justified in matching the punishment to the criminal's entire person. Prison is most apt in this regard. It takes over each inmate's total life.

An Indeterminate Sentence?

Lest this be seen as another form of the indeterminate sentence, we should be clear that this cannot be so if we are to be faithful to Dante's Purgatory. There is hope in Purgatory and it is assumed that eventually all will go through to the top of the mount into Paradise. In fact, Dante even spoke of matching particular amounts of time in Purgatory to the amount of time spent as a sinner on earth. Without this limitation on punishment, it would be a punishment the same as Hell, with no hope. By placing finite limits on the duration of punishment, one recognizes that there is hope. Hope, indeed, is the central force underlying atonement. This is why the initial prison term for any criminal should be finite and of long duration—say 15 years.

Prison as Atonement

All of this is based, of course, upon the assumption that the offender undergoing atonement is convinced that what he has done requires atonement, that he is really guilty of an evil act, and in the most severe cases of having led an evil life. If he is not convinced of this, then he is no different from those relegated by Dante to Hell. For it is the unbelievers, pagans and heathens, and especially those blatantly so, for whom Hell is reserved. In the same way, the offender who does not believe in the evil of his act, or at least in the right of the judge to pronounce him convicted of a crime and deserving of punishment—for this offender there is no hope of redemption. His punishment will be eternal and it is for him that we say, "lock him up and throw away the key." . . .

Obviously, prisoners cannot be subjected to the same terrible tortures in prison as Dante dreamed up for Hell and Purgatory. But is is time that we took prison seriously as a punishment, and realized that these few criminals, these bad people, have been sent there for punishment and that is what they should get. The chronic punishment of prison must be made to have some meaning. That meaning must hinge on the criminal's recognition of his crimes. It must require acts of contrition, including acts that respond in a direct way to the sin of the crime.

For example, on the simplest level, it seems morally required that incarcerated murderers should devote their time to saving lives in whatever way possible, and that they should see it as quite deserving that they should risk their lives for others. Their use for risky medical research might well be justified on this basis.

We might also note in passing that the saving of one life to make up for one murder would not be sufficient. We do not try to match the injury to the victim in such a specific way, for this would be merely the reflection of the crime without any analogical or educative function to punishment. The criminal must devote himself to saving many lives, for it is the guilt of his own actions that must be assuaged, not the actual injury to the victim (though of course, it plays a part). In some cases there may simply not be enough time for the most evil of criminals to make up for the guilt of the sins underlying his crimes.

In Conclusion . . .

If we were to develop a prison-intensive system based on the use of prisons in ways outlined in this chapter, and on strictly limiting prison terms to 15 years or more, it can be seen that prisons would become very harsh places indeed. But at least there would be a clear purpose to their harshness, and we would have to take direct and clear responsibility for what happened in them. This is in contrast to today where we have all kinds of excuses for not taking responsibility for the violence and aimlessness of prison life.

The prison-intensive system also means that the decision to incarcerate individuals is going to be very weighty indeed.

Who is going to make these decisions? Is there not a chance that the numbers will take over for both acute and chronic punishments and we will end up in a worse mess than we are in already?

There are ways that we can make extra sure that this does not happen. But in order to show how this might be done, we must first break down another myth about criminal punishment: that it is unbridled discretion of judges that is the evil cause of our crazily confused and inconsistent punishment system.

"Prison reform has been confused with increasing comforts. Many prisons offer more comfort than the U.S. Army."

Prisons Are Too Comfortable

J.J. Maloney

J.J. Maloney was convicted of murder as a teenager. He served thirteen years in the Missouri State Penitentiary for his crime. While in solitary confinement after an escape attempt, he began to write poetry. The book editor of *The Kansas City Star* came across his work and helped him to gain parole in 1972. During the next six years, while Maloney worked as a reporter for *The Star*, he received the American Bar Association's Silver Gavel Award and the Kansas Bar Association's Media Award for a series of investigative articles on Missouri and Kansas prisons. He is the author of two published novels, *I Speak for the Dead*, and *The Chain*. In the following viewpoint, Mr. Maloney explains his radical ideas on prison reform. He believes the level of creature comforts the prisoners have achieved such as job programs, personal belongings in the cells, and other amenities should be abolished, forcing prisoners to serve "hard time."

As you read, consider the following questions:

1. Why does the author believe that increasing prisoners' comforts is counterproductive?
2. Why does the author say there should be "no factories or jobs" in prison?

J.J. Maloney, "The J.B. Factor," *Saturday Review*, November/December 1983. Copyright © 1983 Saturday Review magazine. Reprinted by permission.

The modern prison system developed over a period of two centuries. As long ago as 1831, it was declared a failure. Alexis de Tocqueville said then, after surveying U.S. prisons, "Nowhere was this system of imprisonment crowned with the hoped-for success. It never effected the reformation of the prisoners."

From that point on there has never been a consensus on what a prison should be like, who should go to prison, what prisons can be expected to accomplish, or how they should accomplish it.

Rehabilitation itself is a much abused word. At various times it was thought that solitude was the answer, or backbreaking work, or psychoanalysis, or education, or simply understanding. When all was said and done, none of them worked.

Instead, we need to understand the dual development in prisons of this century: they have become more lenient as sentences have grown longer. At the urging of well-meaning people, prisons have been infused with amenities, ostensibly to make them more humane. They now have liberties such as correspondence and visiting rules that in some states extend to conjugal visits, weekly telephone calls, commissary privileges, furlough programs, radios, televisions, personalized clothing, magazines, extended yard time, beards and mustaches, and private rooms.

These are not available at all prisons, but that is the trend. Prison reform has been confused with increasing comforts. Many prisons offer more comfort than the U.S. Army offered its soldiers in 1959.

Amenities Cloud Judgment

This is one of the primary factors behind the increased length of prison sentences. These amenities have clouded the public's judgment. As people perceive prison becoming luxurious, they assume it will take longer to accomplish punishment and rehabilitation. The true nature of prison, the terrifying underbelly of it, is only visible to the people who are there. Those outside, as well as the convicts, must know that prison is a major deprivation, inconceivable as an alternative to life outside.

We need a simultaneous development: radically shortened sentences and elimination of all amenities. No factories or jobs, thereby cutting off the source of weapons. No commissary: no cigarettes, coffee, or candy bars. This would eliminate gambling, loan sharking, the trappings of success. No personal radios or televisions. No phone calls, unless the phone call is substituted for a visit. Curtailed correspondence and one visit a month.

In this prison convicts would be given overalls, underwear, socks, and tennis shoes. They would have a flexible toothbrush so it couldn't be sharpened into a weapon, a flexible comb, liquid soap, a towel, and toilet paper. They would be allowed one library book in their cells. No personal property whatever, which alone would eliminate half the violence in prison. No one could smoke, which would eliminate fires and reduce lung cancer. Prisoners would spend more time in their cells, as convicts in solitary do now. Convicts hate solitary; it's boring.

At the end of six months, prisoners could enroll in the prison school, which would let them out of their cells four hours a day. They wouldn't have to enroll in school, but given the alternative, most probably would.

Failure to apply themselves in school or disruptive behavior would be grounds for revoking the privilege. Those who didn't go to school would be housed separately to prevent them from harassing or intimidating those who did.

Every moment that a man was out of his cell, he would be under the direct scrutiny of guards. No rapes. No homosexuality. No maneuvering. There would be less guard-on-inmate brutality. Such brutality often springs from fear. In prisons as they are now, the guards are at the mercy of the inmates. In the proposed prison, the guards would know they had total control. A law would mandate imprisonment for any guard who assaults an inmate, except in self-defense. A second law would mandate imprisonment for any prison employee who conceals knowledge of such an assault. Such prisons would have to be of manageable size.

Harsh Prison Hard to Take

A year in such a prison would be like three years in a current prison. Five years would be hard to take. Ten years would be almost too much.

Bob Dix, *Manchester Union Leader*. Reprinted with permission.

The cost factor of such a prison would be higher, because all the food service, school, and hospital employees would be civilians instead of convicts. On the other hand, there would be far fewer people in these prisons, and for shorter periods of time.

The only people who would need to go to prison would be violent, dangerous offenders: killers, rapists, kidnappers, armed robbers. Fifty-three percent of the people now in prison are convicted of non-violent offenses: forgery, embezzlement, non-sufficient funds checks, gambling, prostitution, petty theft, shoplifting, bribery, confidence games, pickpocketing, fraud, pornography, drug use, burglary, car theft, and sex acts between consenting adults.

As a nation we can't afford to send these people to the penitentiary. When a man steals $100 and spends two years in prison—at a cost of thousands of dollars a year—we are committing fiscal folly. The only non-violent crimes that merit a prison term are those in the category of "criminal enterprise": professional forgery rings, burglary rings, fencing operations, and drug rings.

The rest of these people should be treated as misdemeanants, facing a term in a rigorous local jail. Under this kind of setup, it would be necessary for the rural counties to build regional jails, so that no one county would have to maintain such an expensive institution. It might be necessary for the state to bear part of the cost.

What are the logistics of turning the system we now have into the envisioned one? It's easier than you might think. The governor has the power of clemency. He can decree that all people with no violent crimes on their records are to have their sentences reduced to two years, and that all those with two years are to be given 120 days good time. That would open up an enormous amount of prison space in a relatively short time.

The second step is to devise a sentencing structure for all new convicts. An essential ingredient is fairness. The same crime should carry the same penalty for the rich and the poor, black and white, the educated and the ignorant.

Contemporary theory, however, is going in the other direction. The way we do it now, a mildly retarded defendant from a poor family, with little education, is punished much more harshly than an honor student from a good family. The honor student is seen as a potential asset to society, the other defendant as more likely to be a lifelong liability.

Evaluations Needed

Most courts now use "pre-sentence evaluation." When sentencing, they consider the defendant's familial stability, his education, his prior record, his marital status, etc. If the defendant has a good profile, the recommendation may be that he not go to prison at all. The poor defendant I described probably would receive a much longer sentence. A kid from a white-collar family probably would be granted probation the first time around, even for armed robbery. Many people steal knowing they have one free slide coming. By punishing the crime rather than the individual, the courts could eliminate such thinking. It is common in every prison for one man to be serving two years for a crime, and another to be serving twenty years for a similar crime. That is a great source of bitterness. Judicial discretion breeds judicial abuse.

Prisoners' Rights Are Nonsensical

The experts tell us that, because of overcrowding, prisons are not safe. So they have to keep criminals out of jail; well, the reason the prisons are unsafe is because of the experts.

Years ago prison wardens came from the ranks of the prison guards. Prisoners thought thrice before they assaulted guards. Inmates didn't have access to loads of contraband. Furthermore, you didn't have the frequent escapes and riots that plague us today. Prison wardens today are college graduates, in other words, experts. With the help of the courts they've seen to it that prisoners have all kinds of ''rights''—the right to rape, riot, murder, and escape. We don't need money and studies for our prisons; we need to get rid of the experts and start applying some plain old-fashioned common sense.

Walter Williams, *The Washington Times*, March 12, 1985.

Most importantly, once the prisoner had served his time and completed parole, he should be done with it forever. All rights as a citizen should be restored to him. Five years after completion of parole, his criminal record should be expunged.

The current system is obviously not working. It's time to try something radically new.

"Being locked away from one's family and friends, being totally out of control of one's life, is a deprivation that dwarfs the significance of television, stereos, and designer jeans."

Prison Comforts Make Little Difference

John Irwin•and Rick Mockler

John Irwin and Rick Mockler are members of the Prisoners Union, an organization of convicts and ex-convicts that seeks to gain a prevailing wage for all work done in prison, establish a uniform and equitable sentencing procedure and restore civil and human rights to convicts and ex-convicts. The group publishes a monthly newspaper, *The California Prisoner*, from which this viewpoint is taken. The authors write in direct response to J.J. Maloney, the author of the previous viewpoint. They argue that the few creature comforts that prisoners have obtained are inconsequential, and divert the public's attention from the real issue, namely America's over-reliance on imprisonment.

As you read, consider the following questions:

1. How have increased prison comforts hurt prisoners more than helped them, according to the authors?
2. What do the authors believe is the true punitive nature of prison?
3. Do the authors think that making prisons harsher may make them more effective?

John Irwin and Rick Mockler, "Prison 'Comforts': Friend or Foe?: Prisoners Union Response," *The California Prisoner*, June 1984.

Although Maloney's proposal is a bit extreme, it raises a good point: Increasing comforts in recent years have hurt prisoners more than helped them. Physical "comforts," which are arbitrarily available to a small number of prisoners, create the illusion in the public's mind that our prisons are soft.

Part of the reason sentence lengths have increased so dramatically in recent years is the public perception that our prisons are soft. When the Watergate defendants went to prison, for instance, the nation reacted angrily to reports of inmates playing golf and tennis.

California sentence lengths have soared as politicians like Sen. Dan Boatwright have berated prisoner-owned televisions, state-issued designer jeans (Frontera), and a prison swimming pool (Norco). Liberal Democrats questioned the severity of our penal system after observing Dan White's treatment in jail and prison, during which time a conjugal visit provided the Whites with a child.

Public Easily Sidetracked

Because it has such little contact with prisons and prisoners, the public doesn't realize how inconsequential these "comforts" are. The public is sidetracked from the true punitive nature of prison: the deprivation of freedom. Being locked away from one's family and friends, being totally out of control of one's life, is a deprivation that dwarfs the significance of television, stereos, and designer jeans.

The problem is that to outsiders the most tangible aspects of prison life are the externals. Because prisoners are allowed to wear the same clothes, listen to the same music, and play the same sports as people on the outside, the public doesn't appreciate the punitive nature of imprisonment. It has become common for the "liberals" who helped prisoners obtain physical "comforts" to also support increased sentence lengths.

Prisoners and their families often play into this charade by spending their time and energy attempting to make prison comfortable, while allowing law-and-order advocates to build more prisons and lengthen prison sentences. While we haven't polled prisoners on the subject, we suspect many would gladly sacrifice their TVs, stereos, conjugal visits, tennis courts, and personalized clothing in order to shorten sentences and reduce imprisonment.

Another reason to eliminate these comforts is their unequal availability. As Maloney mentions, drug hustling creates small fortunes in prison. Additionally, prisoners with affluent families on the outside can obtain comforts unavailable to the general population. Not only is this unfair to the average prisoner, but it creates an exaggerated impression in the mind of the public.

Conjugal visits are even more trouble. Unavailable to single people and to common-law couples, conjugal visits for married couples are infrequent and often manipulated by prison policy.

Despite this fact, conjugal visits in the past two decades have created the public impression that prisoners are pampered.

Our criticism of Maloney is that he goes too far. Maloney is not simply proposing to eliminate controversial amenities, but to harshen prison in profound and debilitating ways. Maloney asks us to trust him as an ex-convict, that because the medicine tastes bad it must be good for us.

Harsh Prisons Not Effective

There is simply no evidence that making prisons harsher will make them more effective. Truly harsher prisons might just worsen recidivism. Segregated housing often strips prisoners of the social skills they need if they are to succeed on release. Curtailment of visiting and correspondence deprives prisoners of contact with the real world; it erodes precious bonds with family and friends.

Prisoners' Rights a Necessity

To tell guards that they can deprive prisoners of any possessory rights encourages them to treat prisoners as less than individuals. To tell prisoners that they have no right to the undisturbed possession of even non-contraband personal property is to treat them as if they were nothing more than animals. When we permit ourselves to treat any of us as less than human, we are all diminished.

Dennis E. Curtis, *The Los Angeles Times*, July 23, 1984.

Additionally, the public would probably not realize the severity of Maloney's proposals, and so would not be inclined to reduce sentences by the two-thirds Maloney suggests. Since the public doesn't seem to appreciate the severity of locking someone in a regular cellblock, the additional severity of locking someone in solitary would probably not be appreciated either. Since the public isn't too concerned about any kind of visiting other than conjugal, the curtailment of regular visiting probably wouldn't have much impact in the mind of the public.

The creation of "comforts" in prison has sidetracked much of the debate over prisons in recent years. Making an issue of "comforts" has allowed conservatives to push through longer sentences and more prisons. We propose focussing the debate back on society's use/overuse of imprisonment.

Recognizing Stereotypes

"Which are you—a victim of society or a crook?"

Drawing by Ed Arno; © 1979 The New Yorker Magazine, Inc.

A stereotype is an oversimplified or exaggerated description of people or things. Stereotyping can be favorable. However, most stereotyping tends to be highly uncomplimentary and, at times, degrading.

Stereotyping grows out of our prejudices. When we stereotype someone, we are prejudging him or her. Consider the above cartoon: the prisoner's question, while funny, also expresses two common stereotypes of the criminal.

The following statements relate to the subject matter in this chapter. Consider each statement carefully. *Mark S for any statement that is an example of stereotyping. Mark N if the statement is not an example of stereotyping. Mark U if you are undecided about any statement.*

If you are doing this activity as a member of a class or group, compare your answers with those of other class or group members. Be able to defend your answers. You may discover that others will come to different conclusions than you. Listening to the reasons others present for their answers may give you valuable insights into recognizing stereotypes.

If you are reading this book alone, ask others if they agree with your answers. You too will find this interaction very valuable.

S = stereotype
N = not a stereotype
U = undecided

1. A prisoner is treated like a little boy in prison.

2. A person becomes a criminal because of poor upbringing.

3. Prisoners deserve the harsh treatment they receive in prison.

4. No one really knows the reason people commit crimes.

5. Prisons are schools of crime.

6. More blacks than whites are imprisoned.

7. Criminals are criminals, no matter where they are.

8. Criminals can outgrow crime.

9. Juveniles should be put in prison in order to teach them a lesson they will never forget.

10. People are imprisoned for committing crimes.

11. Some criminals don't belong in prison.

12. Putting someone in prison may be worse than allowing he/she to go free.

13. Prisons alter a person's personality.

14. Criminals can be rehabilitated.

15. Society makes people commit crimes.

16. Outdated facilities make crime in prison inevitable.

17. A higher proportion of prisoners came from poor neighborhoods.

Bibliography

The following list of books, periodicals, and pamphlets deals with the subject matter of this chapter.

John F. Alexander	"Society's Crime," *The Other Side*, October 1981.
Bud Allen and Diana Bosta	*Games Criminals Play*, Susanville, CA: Rae Jolm Publishers, 1983.
George M. Anderson	"D.C. Jail: The Crime of Punishment," *America*, May 12, 1984.
George M. Anderson	"American Imprisonment Today," *America*, May 8, 1982.
Jim Andresky	"'Soft' Prisons, There's No Such Thing," *Forbes*, April 23, 1984.
John R. Coleman	"What I Learned Last Summer," *Psychology Today*, November 1980.
Samuel H. Day Jr.	"Behind Candied Bars," *The Progressive*, November 1983.
Nick DiSpoldo	"Notes from a Prison Cell," *America*, May 8, 1982.
Christine Montilla Dorffi	"The Worst Prison System in America," *Reason*, November 1983.
Shelley Douglass	"Jail Break: Why Do We Choose to Live in Jails?" *The Other Side*, May 1984.
Kathleen Engel and Stanley Rothman	"Our Reformed and Violent Prisons," *The Wall Street Journal*, December 12, 1983.
Mark O. Hatfield	"The American Prison System: A Time-Bomb Ticking?" *e/sa*, May 1983.
Murray Hausknecht	"Crime and Culture," *Current*, July/August 1983.
Graeme R. Newman	*Just and Painful: The Case for the Corporal Punishment of Criminals*, New York: Macmillan Publishing Co., 1983.
Stanton E. Samenow	*Inside the Criminal Mind*, New York: New York Times Book Co., 1984.
Anne Farrer Scott	"The Workhouse Was Strangely Like My Grade School," *The New York Times*, November 22, 1984.
John Edgar Wideman	*Brothers & Keepers*, New York: Holt Rinehart & Winston, 1984.

How Should Criminals Be Sentenced?

"Selective incapacitation. . . is in fact a modest proposal for simultaneously confronting the twin demons of high crime rates and large prison populations."

Selective Imprisonment Should Be Used

Brian Forst

Brian Forst is director of research at The Police Foundation, a criminal justice research organization. In the following viewpoint, he supports the criminal sentencing procedure of selective imprisonment, the imprisonment of repeat offenders and dangerous criminals. Selective imprisonment works on the principle that experts can determine which criminals are more likely to commit more crimes and which are not. Those who are more likely to commit crimes are imprisoned for longer periods of time.

As you read, consider the following questions:

1. With selective imprisonment, the author asserts, many who are now in jail would be released. What type of sentencing would they receive?
2. How can selective imprisonment reduce the prison population, according to the author?
3. This type of sentencing is based on predicting future criminal conduct. According to the author, how is future criminal conduct predicted?

Brian Forst, "Selective Incapacitation: a Sheep in Wolf's Clothing?" *Judicature*, October/November 1984. Reprinted with the author's permission.

The latest prominent principle of sentencing is that of "selective incapacitation." Selective incapacitation, like general incapacitation, involves sentencing with the goal of protecting the community from the crimes that an offender would commit if he were on the street. It differs from general incapacitation in its attempt to replace bluntness with selectivity. Under a strategy of selective incapacitation, probation and short terms of incarceration are given to convicted offenders who are identified as being less likely to commit frequent and serious crimes, and longer terms of incarceration are given to those identified as more crime prone.

Crime Reduction Potential

An attractive aspect of the selective incapacitation concept is its potential for bringing about a reduction in crime without an increase in prison populations. This reduction could be substantial. . . .

The concept of selective incapacitation is controversial, however, for two basic reasons. First, it represents a departure from the more traditional purposes of criminal sanctions—retribution, deterrence, and rehabilitation—purposes that have solid philosophical, if not scientifically validated, foundations. Selective incapacitation is controversial, secondly, because its effectiveness is based largely on the statistical prediction of criminality, and such prediction is an imperfect science. The courts have had great difficulty acknowledging the acceptability of a policy in which its actions are based on imperfect predictions of human behavior, despite the fact that actions of the courts are routinely based on such predictions already in the absence of any such acknowledgment.

Is selective incapacitation truly an effective and appropriate proposal, an "idea whose time has come," or is it another criminal justice fad, or worse—a proposal that carries with it a potential for injustice?. . .

Social Justice and Deterrence

Reserving prison and jail space for the most criminally active offenders may in some instances conflict not only with other norms of legal justice, but with norms of social justice as well. Repeat offenders fall basically into two categories: those who are prone to violence and those who are not. If we reserve the sanction of incarceration only for the dangerous repeat offender, excluding the white collar offender and certain other criminals who pose no serious threat of physical injury to others, we may end up permitting harmful people from the middle class to evade a sanction that less privileged offenders cannot. Some white collar offenders, after all, impose greater costs on society than many dangerous street offenders, and it is clearly unjust to allow the former to pay a smaller price for their crimes than the latter must pay. . . .

For many classes of offenders, a short term of incarceration, indeed, may have a substantially larger crime control impact by way of deterrence than by way of incapacitation. Which offenders? Both empirical evidence and common sense point to the white collar and the property crime offender as the ones who are most deterred by criminal sanctions; the violent offender has been found to be less influenced by the threat of a severe sanction.

Prison for the Dangerous Only

Today's jails are crowded with people who are no threat to anyone— tax cheaters, extortionists, confidence men, stock swindlers, and so forth. They do not belong behind bars. The only reason they are in prison is due to an out-dated and discredited theory that jails "rehabilitate" people.

Nonsense. Let them do their time usefully, outside of jail, nothing cushy but something useful.

This is not a "soft" proposal at all. The dangerous criminals should certainly be shut away. But, today, there often isn't room for the dangerous offender in our overcrowded jails and the dangerous criminal plea-bargains his way back onto the street.

Jeffrey Hart, *The Union Leader*, August 17, 1981.

As long as the offender is a serious, high crime-rate offender, selective incapacitation must obviously be an effective crime control strategy (ignoring crimes against other inmates), regardless of the color of his collar; but it is likely to be a superfluous crime control concept for the offender who is more prone to being individually deterred by a short and usually unpleasant experience in jail or prison . . . .

Effect on Prison Population

What about the prospect of selective incapacitation leading to further prison overcrowding? If, in addition to those who are presently being sent to prison and jail, we were to follow a strategy of incarcerating those with the highest crime-risk profiles, some of whom would not otherwise be incarcerated, then prison and jail populations would indeed be larger than otherwise.

That, however, is not how selective incapacitation works. Under a selective incapacitation strategy, many of those who are currently being incarcerated would receive alternative sanctions—probation with close supervision, the "halfway" house, community service, and so on. Selective incapacitation means reserving prison and jail space for those who are predictably the most criminally active and harmful, subject to maximum and minimum sentence constraints based on offense seriousness. Many who are currently incarcerated would not be under such a strategy. Those who believe strongly in deterrence or just deserts might, indeed, have reason to fear that a strategy of selective incapacitation could cause offenders who they think belong in prison or jail to be released, so that more criminals could go unpunished under that strategy than under other strategies. Thus, larger prison populations might in fact be more closely associated with the deterrence or just deserts strategies than with a selective incapacitation strategy.

It should be obvious that no particular sentencing strategy or mix of strategies is likely to please everyone. Any given prison and jail occupancy level is bound to be too high for some and too low for others. For any given prison population level, however, a selective incapacitation strategy does offer a consistent rationale for attempting to minimize the crime rate.

The Problem of Prediction

One of the most pervasive criticisms of selective incapacitation is that it is based on the statistical prediction of dangerousness; because such predictions are often erroneous, according to this point of view, they should not be used by the court. This criticism is related to both the nature of the errors and to the use of certain information for predicting a defendant's dangerousness.

Let's first consider the nature of errors in prediction. Prediction usually results in some successes and in two kinds of errors: predicting that a phenomenon such as recidivism will occur when in fact it does not ("false positives") and predicting that it will not occur when in fact it does ("false negatives"). The problem of false positives in sentencing is costly primarily to incarcerated defendants who are not really so dangerous, while false negative predictions impose costs primarily on the victims of subsequent crimes committed by released defendants. In predicting whether a defendant will recidivate or "go straight," the problem of false positives is widely regarded as especially serious, for many of the same reasons that it has been regarded in our society as better to release nine offenders than to convict one innocent person....

A tempting alternative is to reject prediction altogether; obviously, if we do not predict, then no errors of prediction are possible. A flaw in this logic is that, whether we like it or not—indeed, even if we tried to forbid it—criminal justice decisions are now, and surely always will be, based on predictions, and imperfect ones, at that. Attempts to discourage prediction in sentencing may in fact produce the worst of both worlds: the deceit of predictive sentencing disguised as something more tasteful, and inferior prediction as well.

If we are to reserve at least some prison and jail space for the most criminally active offenders, then the prediction of criminal activity is an inescapable task....

Selective incapacitation, the latest theory for dealing with crime, is in fact a modest proposal for simultaneously confronting the twin demons of high crime rates and large prison populations. It is less than a universal remedy, first, because our prisons and jails are already populated with many crime prone offenders and, second, because it is not fully consistent with other legitimate reasons to incarcerate some offenders and release others, reasons related primarily to basic principles of justice.

Modest gains, however, are better than none. Continuing frustration with crime on the one hand, and prison and jail overpopulation on the other, suggests a need to exploit modest opportunities whenever they present themselves. Neither the pervasive "career criminal" prosecution programs nor the most touted sentencing guideline systems currently in operation make use of the factors that have been found repeatedly to be associated with repeat criminal behavior. The result is to impose avoidable, and possibly substantial, costs on two groups: offenders who are incarcerated for terms that exceed what can be supported by evidence on how those terms protect the public, and victims of crime committed by released offenders for whom abundant evidence indicates that their release was premature.

Cops and Parole Boards Use It

Some will object to the notion of locking up a 16 year-old rapist or robber for 20 years—until he no longer poses a real threat to the community—by use of a social science derived formula. Yet selective incapacitation has become a working definition for what cops and parole boards are trying to do. In fact, a trickle-down version of the theory—where prosecutors target known career criminals, and judges throw the proverbial book at them—is the best strategy that many communities have devised given scarce resources of cops and prison cells.

Lisa Schiffren, *Policy Review*, Spring 1985.

It is frequently asserted that the public is foolish to insist, simultaneously, on less crime and less taxes for prisons and jails. In fact, less crime may be compatible with less public expenditures on prisons and jails for a variety of reasons. One is the opportunity for prosecutors, judges, and parole boards to make their decisions with a more informed view of the degree of crime risk presented by each defendant.

"Imprisoning an offender because she is dangerous. . . . constitutes an immoral and illegal intrusion upon the individual's freedom."

Selective Imprisonment Should Not Be Used

Lee S. Pershan

Lee S. Pershan is an editor-in-chief of the *New York University Review of Law and Social Change*. In the following viewpoint, Mr. Pershan explains that none of the methods currently used can accurately predict future criminal behavior. People confined under the policy of selective imprisonment may therefore be required to serve unjustly long sentences. Mr. Pershan concludes that it is unlikely that selective imprisonment can provide the benefits that it promises.

As you read, consider the following questions:

1. How does the author prove that predicting criminal behavior is impossible?
2. What does the author mean when he says that selective imprisonment violates the individual's autonomy?
3. How will selective imprisonment affect the crime rate, according to the author?

Lee S. Pershan, "Selective Incapacitation and the Justifications for Imprisonment," *New York University Review of Law & Social Change*, Vol. XII, No. 2, 1983-1984. Reprinted with permission.

Selective incapacitation's opposition to imprisoning the non-dangerous offender makes it a seemingly attractive theory. The proponents of selective incapacitation observe that it is unnecessary to imprison the nondangerous, since by definition the nondangerous offender endangers no one. Therefore, penalization should be reserved for those offenders who are likely to commit violent crimes if they are released. Incapacitating the dangerous, it is argued, is the only way to protect the law-abiding public . . . .

Nevertheless, dangerousness is an inappropriate criterion in sentencing proceedings . . . . It is impossible to predict with any accuracy who is likely to prove dangerous. The courts cannot distinguish the dangerous from the nondangerous. In addition, because the definition of violent crime will undoubtedly exclude most dangerous corporate crime, many dangerous offenders will remain free . . . . Even if it were possible to identify the dangerous offender, it would be impermissible to incarcerate her on the grounds that she was dangerous. Imprisoning an offender because she is dangerous is punishment based on status and future behavior. It constitutes an immoral and illegal intrusion upon the individual's freedom . . . .

Attempts to Identify the Dangerous

The most fundamental practical problem with selective incapacitation is the inability of the courts to determine which offenders are dangerous. Although different approaches . . . have been used, no one has been able to identify the dangerous offender. It is essential to note that the issue here is the prediction of *future* dangerousness, not the assessment of *past* acts. Therefore, even if the sentencing judge knows that the offender was dangerous when she committed the crime for which she is being sentenced, that judge cannot know whether or not the offender remains dangerous and will commit a crime if she is released.

The difficulty in predicting future dangerousness is evident from follow-up studies of offenders who have been diagnosed as dangerous by courts, parole boards, psychiatrists and social workers. In every study, the majority of these supposedly dangerous offenders has failed to act true to form; only a small minority has committed more offenses. Those incorrectly diagnosed (i.e. those who did not, contrary to predictions, commit any more crimes) have invariably outnumbered those correctly diagnosed (i.e. those who upon release did commit more crimes), sometimes by as much as eight to one. Thus, when an offender is incapacitated for being dangerous, most of the time incapacitation is unnecessary—the offender is no longer dangerous. In an extreme case, only 5.2% of a group of supposedly dangerous juvenile offenders offended anew. This is more aptly called "unselective incapacitation." If incarceration is appropriate only for the dangerous, then most imprisoned offenders have been unjustly incarcerated....

If incarceration is to be based on the courts' current ability to predict dangerousness, almost as many dangerous offenders will be released as imprisoned. If the goal of selective incapacitation is to protect the public from the dangerous offender, it is necessary to make more accurate predictions....

Past Actions May Not Be Relevant

Determining that the offender has proven dangerous in the past does not tell the court whether or not the offender currently presents a high risk to the public. There is no logical reason to assume that since the offender has committed a violent crime in the past, she will commit more violent crimes in the future. Such definitions based on past behavior are both too broad—since offenders who are unlikely to offend again are incarcerated along with those who are likely to re-offend—and too narrow, since those offenders who have so far only been convicted of nonviolent crimes will be labelled non-dangerous even if they are highly likely to commit violent crimes in the future....

Selective Imprisonment and the Courts

If psychiatrists and psychologists are ready to concede that they cannot predict which offenders will prove dangerous and which will not, judges who have not had training in prognosticating the future behavior of offenders should not use dangerousness as a factor in sentencing proceedings....

Prediction Is Unpredictable

Predictably, the idea of selective incapacitation is attractive to many politicians and law enforcement people....

But the problems are many and have not begun to be adequately addressed. The theory poses a serious threat to one of the basic precepts of criminal law: innocent until proven guilty. Selective incapacitation metes out punishment for predicted future crimes. And the study of predicted behavior, whether it be violent and dangerous, or merely recidivist, is an inexact science at best.

Jericho, Winter 1982/83.

It is not surprising that courts have had difficulty predicting dangerousness. It is probably impossible to provide a definition of dangerousness that will separate the nondangerous from the dangerous so that a court can determine whether the offender needs to be incapacitated. Classifications must assume that people will invariably act in character, but chance and circumstance lead people to behave out of character. No prediction is perfect. Consequently, attempts to punish on the basis of dangerousness must founder because the court is forced to guess whether or not the offender is dangerous. . . .

No Accurate Predictions

In conclusion, the studies indicate that at present it is impossible to make accurate predictions of dangerousness. For every offender correctly labelled dangerous, at least one offender will be erroneously labelled dangerous. If the number of mistaken predictions of dangerousness is significantly reduced so that the predictions of dangerousness are correct even fifty percent of the time, there will still be several mistaken predictions of nondangerousness for every correct prediction of dangerousness. Nor do the studies offer much hope for improvement. Many conclude that it will never be possible to identify the dangerous. Therefore, since half the dangerous offenders will slip by—they will not be incarcerated—and many nondangerous offenders will be imprisoned mistakenly, bifurcating punishment according to an assessment of dangerousness is unjust. . . .

Selective Incapacitation and the Crime Rate

Although sentencing policies generally are not expected to have any effect on crime rates, proponents of selective incapacitation argue that it should be adopted precisely because it will reduce the crime rate without increasing the prison population. By selectively imprisoning dangerous offenders, the streets will supposedly be made much safer for law-abiding citizens. However, selective incapacitation's effect will not be nearly as great as its proponents suggest. . . .

Incapacitating an individual prevents that person from committing a crime so long as she is imprisoned. However, if the offender is not permanently incarcerated, she is not permanently incapacitated. Most offenders will eventually be released even if they remain dangerous, as the proportionality requirement will usually preclude permanent incapacitation.

Selective incapacitation, therefore, is a practical method of crime prevention only if prisons rehabilitate. Unfortunately, prisons do not (and perhaps cannot) rehabilitate. Rehabilitation is especially unlikely to work in the currently overcrowded and lawless prisons. When the inmate leaves prison, most likely she has not been reformed.

In fact, in many cases prisons make prisoners more dangerous. . . .

If the ordinary (i.e., nondangerous) offender is prepared (or forced by circumstances) to resume a criminal career, it is especially likely that the dangerous offender—who was incarcerated precisely because it was certain that she would commit a violent

100

crime if she was not imprisoned and who was not paroled because she remained dangerous—will soon offend again. In fact, if she did not, the assessment of dangerousness would have been wrong, and the premise upon which incapacitation was justified would be invalid. . . .

Violent Crime Will Not Cease

With selective incapacitation violent crime will not cease. Many violent crimes are committed by people with no record of violence. Under a selective incapacitation scheme at the time of this violent offense they would not have been incapacitated since, if they had previously committed any crimes, those crimes would be minor ones. Nor, if they are unlikely to commit more violent crimes in the future, will they be incarcerated for this crime. . . .

Selective incapacitation may actually lead to an increase in crime. If one believes that offenders are deterred by the certainty of punishment, especially the certainty of imprisonment, selective incapacitation is counterproductive since the likelihood of imprisonment decreases. The offender, who currently does not know if she will be caught, or prosecuted, or convicted, will face one more uncertainty: she will not know whether she will be labelled dangerous or nondangerous. Because fewer offenders will be imprisoned, offenders may be readier to commit crimes. . . .

The Selective Imprisonment Myth

We do not know whether keeping certain convicted robbers and burglars locked up will have any impact on the rates of robbery and burglary. Nonetheless, the return of [this] old myth is getting a lot of attention. It always does, because it is such a convenient answer to the crime problem. It focuses on some of the least powerful persons in the society and makes no demands of the status quo.

John K. Irwin, *The California Prisoner*, May 1983.

Selective incapacitation's rhetoric is direct: rehabilitation did not work, deterrence did not work, retribution is not working. Therefore, only selective incapacitation is left; let's try it. . . . Selective incapacitation is founded upon despair; it is the proposal of a bankrupt. The proponents have retreated to the position that even though the threat of imprisonment will not deter people outside prison, not even those who have just been released, and even though incarceration does not reform criminals, imprisonment is beneficial. It is beneficial not because of any satisfaction that law-abiding citizens may obtain when they hear the news that an offender is to be deprived of her liberty and locked in a cell with other equally vile offenders, but merely because while the offender is locked behind bars, she cannot commit any more crimes.

Incapacitating offenders, however, must also be rejected as a justification for incarceration. Because the dangerous offender cannot be identified, incapacitation will prove unselective. There will be either arbitrary incapacitation or general (i.e., total) incapacitation. The implementation of selective incapacitation is unlikely to reduce prison overcrowding or reduce the cost of running prisons. Because selective incapacitation punishes for future acts, implementation of this theory may be unconstitutional and it clearly is incompatible with the right of autonomy. Nor is it evident that it will reduce street crime. . . .

A careful analysis suggests that selective incapacitation should be rejected. First, it is impossible to identify the dangerous offender. As a result, either the vast majority of offenders are imprisoned to insure that all dangerous offenders are incarcerated or a small number of offenders is imprisoned so that most of the non-dangerous offenders will not be imprisoned mistakenly. If the former policy is followed, the prison population will rise and overcrowding will increase. If the latter policy is followed, many dangerous offenders will not be imprisoned and, if the proponents of selective incapacitation are correct, the crime rate should rise.

Moreover, any attempt to make imprisonment turn on a finding of dangerousness involves ethical and constitutional difficulties. The dangerous offender is imprisoned not for her past acts, but for her predicted future acts and for being "dangerous." Since one cannot be punished for one's status or for still-unattempted acts, selective incapacitation rests on constitutionally infirm ground. Moreover, the offender's autonomy is denied when she is told that she will commit a crime, despite all her protests to the contrary.

Finally, it seems unlikely that selective incapacitation can provide the benefits that it promises. The crime rate is unlikely to go down. The prison population will remain at least as large as it is today.

"Victims . . . should be consulted about charges, plea bargains and tactics."

Crime Victims Should Participate in Sentencing

Louise Gilbert

A relatively recent development in criminal sentencing is the participation of crime victims in all aspects of the sentencing process: bail, original court sentence, and future parole and probational hearings. In the following viewpoint, Louise Gilbert gives a powerful first-hand account of the brutal murders of her son and daughter-in-law and her own abortive attempt to be involved in the legal proceedings against the killer. In doing so, she makes a strong case for allowing crime victims' testimony.

As you read, consider the following questions:

1. Do you feel that Ms. Gilbert was treated justly by the criminal justice system? Why or why not?
2. Why does Ms. Gilbert believe that she should have been allowed to participate in the sentencing of her son's murderer?

Louise Gilbert, "And the Judge Cried Too," *Newsweek*, May 28, 1984. Copyright 1984, by Newsweek, Inc. All rights reserved. Reprinted by permission.

The scene is a tree-lined main street in a small Southern town. It is deceptively quiet. My family and I are the only strangers. We are victims. I am a victim of the violent murder of my son and daughter-in-law.

Andy and Pamela moved from suburban Philadelphia south, from manicured lawns to an 80-acre farm with a log house in need of restoration. They had seen those peaceful hills on their honeymoon only one year earlier and decided it was the perfect place to raise children and build their lives. Their dreams ended on June 24, 1981. Pam was beaten, raped and shot, wrapped in a blanket and buried in the cistern behind their house. That night Andy was shot in the back of the head. The man who would subsequently be charged with their murders was an acquaintance of theirs.

The first trial was scheduled for October and postponed, rescheduled for December. I had to go. It was my responsibility to represent Andy and Pam. I would be evidence of their having been alive and loved. The trial was postponed again at the request of the defense. It became apparent we, as parents, had no legal identity.

Decomposing Bodies

Finally in February we sat, with my eldest son, in a small courtroom. I met the prosecutor and moments later came face to face with the man charged with killing my children. During the trial, I learned the full meaning of horror as their last hours were never again left to my imagination. Pam's fractured head and almost nude body were described in detail as well as the size of the maggots and flies that covered her. I bolted the courtroom when the pathologist began to describe my son's bloated body.

The courtroom was a battlefield, combat played out between lawyers and judge with a calm defendant dressed in his best. In life Andy and Pam were young and hopeful, in love with life and each other. Their home was an investment in the future, left half completed. To the defense it was a rough cabin in the woods, a dark question asked over and over: "Why were they there?"

Pam's blood was found in the back of the accused's car. His body, head and pubic hair were found on the blanket in which she was wrapped. After being identified near the scene of the crime the day they were killed, he gave out this story: he and Pam were having an affair. Who could dispute this? Not Pam. More than 90 pieces of evidence were introduced by the prosecution. The defense attacked the method of investigation. Out for three days, the jury reported a deadlock; courtroom gossip had it at 11-1 for conviction. A new trial date was set for August 1982.

Planning for the second trial became our obsession. This time we hired an attorney to represent us. She wanted transcripts. We spent a small fortune to transcribe 1,600 pages of testimony. Meanwhile, the prosecutor lost his bid for re-election and the trial was postponed. We paid for our attorney to go south to discuss the case.

Reprinted by permission. Tribune Media Services Inc.

With the same evidence and witnesses, the case was presented differently. I thought it was a good prosecution and a good jury. But then, after two days of deliberations, an emotional jury returned to the courtroom. It was hopelessly deadlocked. One old man said he had not heard all the evidence: he had a "hearing problem," something he did not mention before the alternates were discharged. Some jurors sobbed: the newspaper reported that even the judge choked back tears. A mistrial was declared and a new trial date was set.

We are financially secure but not wealthy. Preparations to attend these trials were made at great inconvenience and expense. We were at the mercy of schedules made, broken and remade. I was depressed, anxious and in therapy.

Finally, more than two years after the murders, the third trial began in the same courtroom, in the same small, rural community that had been subjected to rumors about my children. By law, a change of venue is left to the discretion of the defense.

Andy and Pam were lost to us, and their character and dignity were lost in the courtroom. Because of the system, the prosecutor was never allowed to be an advocate for them and the defense attorney's attacks were never answered. The trial was over in five days. This time the jury was out and back in what seemed like an hour. Their verdict: not guilty.

Justice System Failed

The case is still open, but it is over for us. The structure of our family was blown apart. Piece by piece we are trying to put ourselves together. I belong to Parents of Murdered Children. Our stories are different but the agony is the same. One pattern is repeated again and again: for us the criminal-justice system has failed to work.

The parents, spouse and children of a murder victim are victims too, and their willingness to become involved should be shored up with legislation and changes in court practice. Victims should have a say in choice of venue and whether hearing dates are continued. Victims should be given free copies of court transcripts. They should be consulted about charges, plea bargains and tactics. They should be informed of the progress of the case. If all else fails, they should be provided with a legal advocate who is permitted to defend the character and the integrity of the dead.

My rights as a parent were no less important than the defendant's. I was victimized by the murder of my children. Then the system victimized me again.

4 VIEWPOINT

"In some instances crime victims—and the organized groups supporting their cause—have resorted to tactics designed to control and intimidate the justice system."

Crime Victims Should Not Participate in Sentencing

Wilbert Rideau and Billy Sinclair

The Angolite is one of the best inmate prison publications in the nation. It is published by the inmates of the Louisiana State Penitentiary in Angola, Louisiana, and is edited by lifers Billy Sinclair and William Rideau. In the following viewpoint, the editors of *The Angolite* believe that crime victims' participation in criminal sentencing borders on the vengeful. Rather than seek justice, crime victims merely try to sway judges and juries toward longer sentences.

As you read, consider the following questions:

1. Why do the authors believe that crime victims do not act responsibly?
2. What are the authors trying to prove when they cite the case of Tony Cimo?
3. What danger do crime victims groups pose, according to the authors?

Wilbert Rideau and Billy Sinclair, "Victims and Vigilantism," *The Angolite*, July/August 1983. Reprinted with permission.

Too often in the past victims of crime have been neglected and even abused by the workings of the criminal justice system. However, in recent years crime victims, as well as their families and supporters, have been more assertive of their interests, carving out a legitimate role in the justice system. But in some instances crime victims—and the organized groups supporting their cause— have resorted to tactics designed to control and intimidate the justice system rather than make it function properly and equitably.

In Detroit Judge Charles Kaufman presided over the trial of two men, Ronald Ebens and his stepson Michael Nitz, who were charged in connection with the beating death of Vincent Chin. Chin was beaten to death with a baseball bat outside a suburban Detroit tavern where he had been celebrating his coming marriage. Ebens and Nitz, both of whom are blue collar workers with no prior criminal history, entered into a plea bargain and pled no contest to a charge of manslaughter. They were fined $3,780 each and placed on three years probation.

Refusing to Buckle

There was an immediate outrage by Chin's family who felt the sentence was too lenient. A group called American Citizens for Justice, a group composed mainly of Asian-Americans, organized a protest rally against Kaufman, demanding that he change the sentence and jail Ebens and Nitz. Despite the protests and criticisms, Kaufman refused to buckle under the demands, saying in a written opinion: "While sympathizing with the family and community of the victim, it is the obligation of the court to decide the matters in accordance with the mandate of law."

But in Denver Judge Alvin Lichtenstein couldn't handle the pressure of protest. He had sentenced Clarence Burns to serve two years in a work-release program for the shooting death of his wife, Patti. In sentencing Burns, Lichtenstein stipulated that he could continue working at his $850-a-month job and would serve his sentence at nights and on weekends in jail so that he could support his teenage son. The sentence stirred such a storm of protest that even Gov. Richard Lamm injected himself in the storm of controversy by calling the sentence "an outrage" and his wife added that the sentence meant women in Colorado are nothing more than property.

What particularly incensed some of the protesters, especially the women's groups, was Lichtenstein's unfortunate remark that Mrs. Burns helped "provoke" her own death by pretending her marriage was stable. As the noise of the crowd pounded in his ears, Lichtenstein changed the sentence to four years in prison, saying that he had been misled by lawyers. Even the stiffer sentence was criticized by the women's groups, prosecutors and defense attorneys.

Lichtenstein justified his change of mind by saying that he learned that Mrs. Burns had left her son nearly $100,000 in assets.

108

That "eliminates the very foundation on which the (original) sentence was imposed," Lichtenstein told Burns. "Neither the prosecution nor your lawyers informed me before I imposed sentence that this large sum of money was available to your son for his immediate support and for his college education. Quite frankly, I believe the court was misled."

Caving into Pressure

David Wyman, Burns' public defender, objected to the sentence, saying that Lichtenstein caved in to "continuing pressure from the media and the public."

Victims Trespass on Criminal Rights

Victims' rights do not have to trespass on the civil liberties of us all. Without absolving the individual perpetrator from his/her actions, society must also be held accountable for the environment in which such crimes are committed. Alternatives to incarceration can emphasize the rights of the victim alongside the responsibility of the offender. But the community must be willing to create and implement such alternatives.

Efforts aimed at making the defendant suffer to the same extent as did the victim is not justice. It is the voice of angry and scared people who do not feel that they have been heard. Furthermore, it is only too easy for the Right to capitalize on the emotions generated by the movement for victims' rights.

Jericho, Spring 1983.

A group in Houston called CRIME (Crime Reduction Involvement Means Education) tried to intimidate Judge Woody Densen. Supporters of the group placed at least 100 calls to the court saying that they wanted 18-year-old Tyrone Carmouche, a convicted burlgar, to be given a stiff sentence. Defense counsel Howard Stripling moved for a mistrial, arguing that his constitutional rights had been violated by CRIME's efforts to influence the judge's sentence. Following a hearing on the motion, Densen ordered a new trial and removed himself from the case, saying that he could no longer be fair and impartial in the case. "This group adversely affects the criminal justice system," Densen said from the bench. He called upon the press, defense lawyers and prosecutors to look into the methods employed by that group, charging that the group seems to target certain judges and conducts itself like a political organization. . . .

Public distrust of the criminal justice system, especially the role of the courts, has spawned law-and-order and court monitoring groups throughout the country. Judges, lawyers, and even some prosecutors are growing uneasy with the pressure tactics being utilized by these groups to impose their concepts of justice on the system. Despite warnings by lawyers and judges that it could clog the courts and perhaps be eventually declared unconstitutional, voters in California last year approved by 56 percent to 44 percent a referendum popularly known "as the crime victim's bill of rights." California is also the state that produced MADD—Mothers Against Drunken Drivers—which now has 153 chapters with 75,000 members across the country. At a recent meeting of 20 Municipal Court Judges in San Francisco it was disclosed that the San Mateo chapter of MADD was monitoring their courtrooms. . . .

It is not so much that judges, lawyers and prosecutors are intimidated by the presence of the groups in the courtrooms, but that they feel the groups should conduct themselves responsibly. Some members of these groups do not know how to criticize responsibly; they wish to set themselves up as divine arbitrators of right and wrong and forcefully impose their views, often articulated with reckless abandon, upon the justice system. They enter the courtroom with presupposed notions as to the guilt of the accused—and once guilt is established through a formal verdict, they expect a harsh and quite often maximum sentence without the benefit of the sentencing information a judge has. . . .

Out for Revenge

A basic problem with the organized monitoring groups is that they fashion their concepts of justice in their living room meetings; concepts which are not thought out or well-reasoned. These groups are primarily angry and dissatisfied with the justice system, but rather than seek changes of the system through the elective and legislative process, they seek to change the system through pressure and intimidation.

Of course, an underlying danger in these groups is that their actions will spark a Tony Cimo—a man who waited four years for the State of South Carolina to execute the killer of his parents before he took the law into his own hands. The justice system moved too slowly for Cimo's concept of justice—he wanted immediate revenge, and when he didn't get it, he hired convicted mass murderer, Donald "Pee Wee" Gaskins, to place a booby-trapped intercom in the death cell of Rudolph Tyner, the killer of Cimo's parents. Tyner was killed when Gaskins detonated the intercom. "It had to be done," the 36-year-old Cimo said. "It's something that should have been done."

At his sentencing Assistant Solicitor Richard Harpootlian said: "Tony Cimo is a tragic figure. He's even more tragic now." Judge James Morris, before passing sentence, said, "People cannot take the law into their own hands."

That fact did not disturb a lot of law-abiding citizens who hailed Cimo as a folk hero. "We've had a bunch of phone calls from all over," Cimo said. "Everyone has been sympathetic...well-wishers. They all feel the same way I do...."

Stirring Up Anger and Frustration

And therein lies the basic danger of monitoring groups—they stir frustration and resentment against the justice system which can prompt the irresponsible individual to take the law into his own hands. America has a lynch-law history; it's an evil that lurks in its soul and Cimo is an expression of the evil, something Wolfe called a "naked worship of brute force." The Cimos want to impose their own concepts of justice with brute force; theirs are the disguised voices of barbarians. They want to dismantle the orderly process of justice; they want to respond to murder with murder. More than a tragic figure, Cimo is a dangerous symbol—he is a murderer as much as Rudolph Tyner was a murderer and ten million well-wishing calls will not erase that fact—it simply bespeaks the dangerous and disturbing trend which is now attacking the very fabric of our justice system.

Distinguishing Between Fact and Opinion

This activity is designed to help develop the basic reading and thinking skill of distinguishing between fact and opinion. Consider the following statement as an example. "Overcrowding is a serious problem in many of America's prisons." This statement is a fact with which few women, men, or government officials would disagree. But consider a statement which attributes prison overcrowding to poverty. "The increase in poverty has driven more people into criminal activity—leading to an increase in prison overcrowding." Such a statement is clearly an expressed opinion. A poor person who has robbed a grocery store to feed his family may agree with this statement, but another equally poor person holding a full-time job may resent the assumption that the poor turn to crime.

When investigating controversial issues it is important that one be able to distinguish between statements of fact and statements of opinion.

The following statements are taken from the viewpoints in this chapter. Consider each statement carefully. *Mark O for any statement you feel is an opinion or interpretation of facts. Mark F for any statement you believe is a fact.*

If you are doing this activity as a member of a class or group, compare your answers with those of other class or group members. Be able to defend your answers. You may discover that others will come to different conclusions than you. Listening to the reasons others present for their answers may give you valuable insights in distinguishing between fact and opinion.

If you are reading this book alone, ask others if they agree with your answers. You too will find this interaction very valuable.

O = opinion
F = fact

1. Prison sentences are for punishment.
2. Selectively imprisoning criminals can reduce crime.
3. A small percentage of criminals commit a large percentage of crime.
4. Selective incapacitation means reserving prison and jail space for those who are the most criminally active and harmful.
5. It is impossible to predict which criminals will commit more crimes.
6. Criminal sentencing, as it is practiced now, involves a lot of guesswork.
7. It is impossible to have less crime and fewer prisons.
8. Imprisoning dangerous offenders because they are dangerous is immoral and illegal.
9. Incapacitating criminals, or making sure they won't commit more crimes by locking them up, should not be a purpose of prison.
10. Privately-operated prisons can save money.
11. Restitution is an alternative to prison.
12. There are about two dozen privately-operated prisons in the US.
13. Criminals should suffer as much as their victims.
14. Crime victims may feel vengeful toward the criminals who victimized them.
15. Society must punish murderers.
16. Crime victims can stir frustration and resentment against the justice system.
17. Corporal punishment is used in many third world countries.
18. Electric shock is a more humane punishment than prison.
19. Laboratory research on rats has shown that electric shock is an effective punishment.
20. Chronic pain is not as effective as acute pain.
21. The military needs men, and society needs new solutions to prison overcrowding.
22. Military conscription can aid criminals' reintegration into society.
23. Restitution has been employed throughout history.
24. Restitution is less restrictive than imprisonment.

Bibliography

The following list of books, periodicals, and pamphlets deals with the subject matter of this chapter.

Jan M. Chaiken and Marcia R. Chaiken	*Varieties of Criminal Behavior*, Santa Monica, CA: The Rand Corporation, 1982.
Congressional Digest	"Federal Criminal Sentencing Policy," June/July 1984.
Francis J. Flaherty	"Crime and Punishment," *The Progressive*, September 1984.
Peter W. Greenwood	*Selective Incapacitation*, Santa Monica, CA: The Rand Corporation, August 1982.
Kenneth Guentert	"Stop Punishing Criminals," *U.S. Catholic*, June 1983.
Robert Hanley	"Listening to the Woes of the Victimized," *The New York Times*, October 23, 1984.
Philip W. Harris	"Sentencing Alternatives: Development, Implementation, Issues and Evaluation," *Judicature*, December/January 1985.
Arthur Johnson	"A Barometer of Violence," *Macleans*, March 5, 1984.
Gaylen Moore	"The Beast in the Jungle," *Psychology Today*, November 1983.
Newsweek	"Giving Victims a Say in Court," March 14, 1983.
	"Sentence by Public Opinion," March 5, 1984.
Prison Fellowship	"Liberty to the Captives," *The Other Side*, December 1981.
Science News	"Predicting Dangerousness: Future Imperfect," June 9, 1984.
Society	"Setting Prison Terms," July/August 1984.
Jackson Toby	"A Higher Price for Lesser Crimes," *The Los Angeles Times*, February 24, 1984.
U.S. News & World Report	"When Convicted Killers Walk Free," January 16, 1984.
	"Crime Victims Ask for Their Day in Court," February 7, 1983.

What Are the Alternatives to Prison?

"Probation's most basic need is for resources to meet its responsibilities."

Probation Can Work

Joan Petersilia

In a 1985 study by the Rand Corporation of adult felons on probation, results showed that a full 75% of these convicts committed
new crimes while on probation. In the following viewpoint, the
author argues that these astounding statistics should not be used
to condemn probation. Rather, what probation needs is more financial and institutional backing in order to fully realize its potential.
Joan Petersilia is a senior researcher in the Rand Corporation
criminal justice program and was director of the original study.

As you read, consider the following questions:

1. According to the author, what types of attitudes and policies
   harm probation?
2. What type of criminals do probation officers primarily deal
   with, according to the author? Does this represent a change?

Joan Petersilia, '"The Probation Time Bomb: 'Get Tough' Justice Doesn't Follow Through
to the Streets," *The Los Angeles Times*, February 3, 1985. Reprinted with the author's
permission.

The Rand Corporation has just published the results from a study that I directed of adult felons in California who have been granted probation. Unfortunately, a misreading of these results could bring a storm of public criticism down on probation agencies—a storm that is not justified.

Rather than castigating probation, critics should realize that these findings actually indict the attitudes and policies that have placed unrealistic and overwhelming demands on probation agencies.

Granted, the study contains some alarming facts about probation as a sentence for felons. Over a 40-month period, our research tracked 1,672 men convicted of felonies and sentences to probation in Los Angeles and Alameda counties. Of that total, 65% were again arrested; 51% of them were convicted, and 34% ended up in jail or prison. Worse, the crimes that they committed were serious—75% of the charges filed against them were for burglary, assault and robbery.

Inadequate Resources at Fault

Probation officials are under fire to explain why they have not been able to curb the criminal behavior of the felons placed under their care. Our study shows that they do not lack either commitment or energy. Rather, their efforts are hampered by inadequate resources and the lack of a clear mandate that would help them make the best use of the resources they have.

Prison crowding is a matter of common knowledge and concern, but relatively few people know that probation is equally overburdened. There are four times as many probationers as prisoners in the United States, and their numbers are growing 30% faster.

This increased use of probation has occurred in the face of waning public and financial support. Although some people believe that probation is the best hope for effective and humane corrections, others want it abolished, asserting that it neither rehabilitates nor controls offenders. Probation is commonly seen as lenient and, thus, out of step with the public's current zeal for harsher penalties. As a result, most probation agencies have had their budgets cut, even as their caseloads are expanding.

Since 1975, California has spent 30% more on criminal justice in general, but 10% less on probation. Last year alone, California courts sentenced 30,000 more people to probation than the year before—an 11% increase—with virtually no increase in dollars to support their supervision. These people simply have to be "absorbed" by already scanty probation resources.

Probation Remains Only Choice

The future looks even grimmer. Prison overcrowding dictates that probation populations will continue to grow. In California and 30 other states, prisons have become so crowded that the courts have set limits on the number of inmates that may be housed. At the same time, shrinking budgets and political uncertainties preclude building enough new prisons to keep pace with felony convictions. Consequently the courts have had to seek other alternatives; in many jurisdictions, probation is the only choice.

These phenomena have radically changed both the nature and the size of the probation population. Probation officers now supervise offenders who are much more threatening to society than the "petty" criminals that probation was intended to handle. In fact, these lesser offenders are often crowded out of probation and, in effect, may receive no punishment for their crimes.

Probation's Advantages

A major advantage of probation is that it allows the offenders to remain in the community and thereby avoids, in the words of one proponent, "the isolating and labeling effects of commitment to an institution." It also spares convicted persons confinement in conditions that are frequently so dehumanizing that some emerge more prone to violence than before.

George M. Anderson, *America*, April 6, 1985.

In California, two-thirds of convicted felons get probation, and in some counties an individual probation officer will have responsibility for more than 300 offenders. As one chief probation officer commented, "That kind of work volume makes the whole idea of probation a sick joke. No single human can adequately evaluate, report on and supervise over 300 criminals at a given time."

More Supervision Needed

Many probation officers can do no more than give these people a stack of postcards to mail in at required intervals. In these instances, probation actually means freedom, with few constraints and little supervision. Today's probationers, who appear to pose a more serious threat to public safety than in the past, should have more supervision, not less.

To compound the problem, California probation agencies historically have served as catch-alls for any tasks that could be tenuously related to their mission. Because they are charged with "preventing delinquency," they perform such disparate and demanding tasks as reviewing school attendance and providing consent for minors to marry, and for step-parent adoptions and custody following divorce. Such tasks divert considerable resources from supervision of offenders, and weaken the probation agencies' ability to make public safety their highest priority.

The current troubles are self-perpetuating. Without some sanction that is intermediate in severity between incarceration and probation for serious offenders, prison populations will continue to grow and the courts will be forced to consider probation for more and more serious offenders. Probation caseloads will increase, petty offenders will be increasingly ignored by the system (possibly creating more career criminals), and recidivism rates will rise. In short, probation appears to be heading toward an impasse, if not a total breakdown, in its ability to supervise offenders adequately.

Ways to Improve Probation

Probation's most basic need is for resources to meet its responsibilities. Increased funding alone will not solve the problem. Probation needs a new mandate that establishes its mission explicitly and recognizes the kind of offenders that it must deal with. The criminal-justice system must recognize that probation's mission has broadened and changed: It is moving away from rehabilitation and toward restrictive supervision. Consequently, the system must alter the responsibilities and structure of probation agencies.

Those responsible for funding have been unwilling to recognize the seriousness of probation's plight. Most counties in California are so financially strapped that reports of another agency "in trouble" fall on deaf ears. But ignoring the problems means that community safety is being jeopardized and that costs are being transferred to other criminal-justice agencies.

Improve, Don't Abandon Parole

The Rand report contains current information on the depth of probation's plight—responsibilities, caseloads, dollars and offender characteristics. Instead of allowing the rearrest rates to be used against them, probation officials should take an active stance and emphasize the "costs" of current policies. They should enumerate for the public and for policy-makers the number of new crime victims, the amount of police and court resources spent on "failed" probations, and the ultimate rise in prison populations—all of which result from the lack of a clear mission and resources for supervising felony probationers adequately.

"Prison serves one valuable purpose: to isolate the offender from society, which...prevents him from committing new crimes during that time."

Probation Cannot Work

Stephen Chapman

Citing the 1985 Rand Corporation study referred to in the previous viewpoint, Stephen Chapman, a nationally syndicated columnist, comes to a different conclusion. He believes the study justifies more imprisonment. Since there is no way to prevent criminals from committing crimes, Mr. Chapman argues, then society owes it to the public at large to lock up these criminals, instead of releasing them on probation.

As you read, consider the following questions:

1. What is the author's solution to prison overcrowding?
2. Do you agree with the author when he says we cannot rehabilitate criminals, merely stop them from committing more crimes? Why or why not?
3. What encourages lawlessness, according to the author?

Stephen Chapman, "Coming to Terms with Probation," *The Washington Times*, January 29, 1985. Reprinted by permission: Tribune Media Services.

For years, the debate has raged over how convicted criminals should be dealt with—by stiff prison terms or by less punitive alternatives like probation.

The latest evidence argues against probation, which is bad news, given the high proportion of offenders who now avoid prison. But there is good news, too—the nation's new willingness to send criminals to prison.

The information comes from a study by the Rand Corporation, which examined 1,672 men convicted of felonies and given probation in Los Angeles and Alameda counties. (Probation, which substitutes for a prison term, shouldn't be confused with parole, which shortens one that has been partly served.) The results are a forceful indictment of probation.

Two-Thirds Rearrested

Two-thirds of the felons were rearrested within 40 months; more than half were convicted of new crimes. Nor were the offenses trivial. Fully 75 percent of them involved burglary, theft, or robbery. Worse, nearly one-fifth of all the probationers were eventually convicted of violent crimes.

The figures are worse than they sound. The criminals given probation are usually the "better" ones—those without prior records or a history of drug use or a penchant for serious violence. These are the offenders who should be best able to function in the straight world. Despite the factors working in their favor, only one of every three men in this study was able to stay out of trouble for a mere 40 months.

This revelation should help to scotch the notion that some felons are not dangerous to society and that judges can reliably gauge which ones they are. Most people who are convicted of crimes apparently will commit more if given the chance.

Most judges probably know that. But they rely on probation because they have little choice. Prison capacity is already strained, so cells must be reserved for the worst offenders. From 60 percent to 80 percent of criminal offenders get probation rather than prison.

Putting Criminals Away

Putting criminals in prison is no panacea either. Recidivism among former inmates is common. But prison serves one valuable purpose: to isolate the offender from society, which (besides punishing him for his transgression) prevents him from committing new crimes during that time. Given the record of these probationers, that means preventing a lot of crimes.

But offenders can't be sent to prison unless there is space for them, and prisons are already overcrowded. Federal prisons hold nearly 33,000 inmates, nearly a third more than they are designed to hold. At the end of 1983, state prisons held 399,072 inmates, about 9 percent more than their stated capacity. Eighteen states,

Bill Deore, *The Dallas Morning News*, reprinted with permission.

strapped for space, have to put some prisoners in local jails.

Fortunately, prison capacity has expanded dramatically in recent years, else the problem would be much worse. The total prison population has risen by 50 percent in the last decade. The federal Bureau of Prisons says it is in the middle of the biggest construction program in its history.

Provide More Prisons

Equally heartening is that legislatures are limiting the latitude of other authorities in meting out punishment. Illinois, like several other states, has adopted "determinate sentencing," which abolishes parole. Once sentenced, an inmate can reduce his term only through good behavior—a necessary device for maintaining prison order. Several states have adopted either minimum sentences for specific offenses or stricter sentencing guidelines.

But the only way to make changes like these work is to provide enough prisons for all the criminals who belong there. Even with the recent expansion, the number of probationers is growing faster than the number of inmates.

That is a sure way to promote lawlessness. Someday, we may discover how to prevent people from turning to crime, or to redeem them once they do. Until then, we owe it to those victimized or threatened by crime to lock the criminals away for a while.

"Private operation of correctional facilities can realize significant cost savings for governments and eliminate a considerable administrative burden as well."

Privately Operated Prisons Are Economical

Robert W. Poole Jr.

Robert W. Poole Jr. is president of the Reason Foundation, an organization that promotes individual philosophy and free market principles. The idea of allowing the private sector to run state and federal programs is not new. The idea is relatively new, however, in the prison system. A few prisons in the United States are privately run, and advocates believe they are more economical and more innovative with prison reforms. In the following viewpoint, Mr. Poole agrees with these advocates.

As you read, consider the following questions:

1. What advantages does the author say privately run prisons have?
2. According to the author, what types of detention facilities are now owned privately?
3. Why is innovation unlikely in government owned institutions, according to Mr. Poole?

Robert W. Poole, Jr., "Rehabilitating the Correctional System." Reprinted, with permission, from the July 1983 issue of FISCAL WATCHDOG. Copyright 1983 by the Reason Foundation, Box 40105, Santa Barbara, CA 93140-0105.

Suppose for a moment that jails, prisons, halfway houses, detention homes and other correctional facilities were owned and operated by private firms.

Corrections authorities would shop around for a facility or facilities in which to place their prisoners. They would compare the services, track records and prices of the various competitors and choose those that best suited their demands. Governments would then simply pay the firms a fee for their services. Under this arrangement, governments would be relieved of the costly burden of building and administering these facilities. And competition would compel firms to try aggressively to satisfy their customers.

Unfortunately, that imaginary time has yet to come. But several developments heading in that direction are now afoot.

Since 1979, for example, the Federal Bureau of Prisons has contracted out all of its halfway-house operations—now 300 or so—to private for-profit firms and nonprofit agencies. Several states, too, contract out some or all of their halfway-house programs. The Immigration and Naturalization Service contracts out some of its lockup facilities (including a 400-bed facility in the Southwest that recently went out for bid). And nationwide, there are some 30,000 juvenile offenders housed in nearly 1,500-privately run facilities.

Private operation of correctional facilities can realize significant cost savings for governments and eliminate a considerable administrative burden as well.

Connecticut's Halfway Houses

Connecticut, for example, contracts out all of its halfway-house operations, and according to Ed Quinlan of the state's Department of Corrections, it would cost the government at least one-third more to run these operations itself. And Art McDonald of Eclectic Communications, Inc.—a southern California-based for-profit firm—reports that ECI operates a juvenile facility in northern California for the Federal Bureau of Prisons—in which inmates are locked up and guarded—for less than half the government's cost.

But reduced cost is not the only benefit of private operation of correctional facilities. Innovation in service and programs is another equally important outcome.

For example, Associated Marine Institutes, which runs the Florida Environmental Institute—a facility for "serious" juvenile offenders—has implemented a unique four-phase program that increases the young offenders' privileges based on good behavior.

The youths start out working at a wilderness camp and, step-by-step, graduate to a city job. And in the operations of halfway houses, styles of administration vary widely from one facility to another. Some emphasize community involvement, for instance, while others may stress job training.

Thus far, privatization of corrections has mainly been limited to juvenile facilities and adult support services, such as halfway houses and work furlough centers. The federal, state and local governments are turning over the operation of more and more of these facilities to private groups. And while most contractors are non-profit social-service agencies—there are a number of growing for-profit firms.

McDonald's ECI, for example, has eight contracts in California. And another southern California-based firm, Rube, Inc., has 11 contracts in California and Arizona.

Also of interest is the emergence of Corrections Corp. of America, a Nashville firm partially backed by investors affiliated with Hospital Corp. of America, the nation's largest hospital company. CCA is seeking contracts with state and local governments in several states to operate adult minimum-security facilities. (At this writing, however, no contracts have yet been announced.)

In addition, according to ECI's McDonald, a group of investor-entrepreneurs in northern California are interested in building and operating a private prison and selling its services to various county and state governments. In McDonald's opinion, it is "very possible" that such private prisons may soon come into existence. And the fact that Don Hutto, vice-president of operations for CCA, has been elected president of the American Correctional Association may represent a significant trend within the corrections field.

Indeed, very real pressures are now forcing governments at all levels to reassess the correctional system.

The 1970s saw a boom in prison construction. But with 60 to 80 per cent of all jail and prison cells designated as "overcrowded," governments nationwide are slated to spend at least $10 billion over

© Liederman/Rothco

the next decade to build even more space for prisoners. And according to Anthony Travisono, past president of the American Correctional Association, state and local governments are finding it more and more difficult to raise capital for constructing new jails and prisons.

Moreover, citizen dissatisfaction with the correctional system is rising. The public is alarmed by high rates of recidivism, by jails and prisons that produce repeat offenders whose crimes only get worse.

Indeed, in a speech given to Pace University's graduating students in June, Chief Justice Warren Burger called the nation's penal system a "recall process" that "sends thousands of repeat offenders back to prisons each year." Burger urged reform and innovation, such as turning prisons into factories where inmates could make and sell goods, thereby learning responsible behavior and paying for their keep.

But such innovation, says Rand Corporation's criminal-justice researcher Peter Greenwood, is unlikely in government-run institutions: "Only true innovation will address the larger problem of why our system of incarceration is such a mess. And when you're looking for innovators you don't look to government; you look to business."

Receiving Bonuses

Greenwood suggests, for example, that private-person operators be given bonuses for reducing recidivism rates and charged penalties for prison violence and escapes. Ted Nissen, who runs the for-profit Rube, Inc., thinks that such terms could be part of goverments' contracts with private corrections firms like Rube.

Between 1978 and 1982, the nation's prison population increased by a third. For governments, that sort of growth means a tremendous cost increase: on average, in operating expenses alone, it now costs governments about $11,000 a year to house a single prisoner. And for law-abiding citizens, who ultimately foot all the bills of prisoners and their crimes, the costs are social and psychological, as well as financial.

At the local level, officials now have increasing opportunities to tap the private sector's wealth of creativity and innovation in reforming the corrections system. It is now only a matter of the willingness to do so.

"Helpless men and women have never fared well in the hands of profit-seeking entrepreneurs."

Privately Operated Prisons Are Unjust

Michael Walzer

Michael Walzer describes himself as a "left-wing intellectual." He is an editor of *Dissent* magazine and contributing editor for *The New Republic*. A professor of social science for the Institute of Advanced Studies at Princeton University, Mr. Walzer is also a prolific writer. In addition to regularly published articles in a number of journals, he has written several books, among them *Spheres of Justice: A Defense of Pluralism and Equality* and his most recent, *Exodus and Revolution*. In the following viewpoint, Mr. Walzer argues that while handing prison management over to private firms may be more economical, it may also make prison conditions unjust. Whereas federal and state prisons must comply with regulations, there is currently no way to keep track of conditions in private prisons. Prisoners' rights, not economy, should govern the prison decision, he concludes.

As you read, consider the following questions:

1. According to the author, what is "wrong with private prisons"?
2. An argument for private prisons is that they will be more competitive than their state and federal counterparts. The author believes this is inaccurate. Why?

Michael Walzer, "Hold the Justice," *The New Republic*, April 8, 1985. Reprinted by permission of *The New Republic*, © 1985, The New Republic, Inc.

There are now some two dozen privately owned and run prisons in the United States, and the number is likely to double in the next year or so. The idea of "privatization," . . . has evidently taken hold—and it has taken hold in a strange place. One somehow imagined that even a minimal state, stripped of all its welfare functions, would still have a police force and a prison system of its own. But private prisons, so the argument goes, are much cheaper to run than public prisons, and the owners can still make a profit; we need such men and their good works. Here are our convicts: *enrichissez-vous!*

We ought to be talking about the barbarous conditions that exist in many prisons, the swelling population of young and minor offenders, alternative forms of custody and control. But the argument from cheapness, in these mean times, is not surprising; it may even be true. Entrepreneurs in the incarceration business will probably be bound by less rigorous building and safety codes; they won't have to pay union wages and pensions; they will more easily skimp on the training of guards and the care of (more and more) prisoners. But if all this makes for economic efficiency, what does it do to justice?

I am inclined to concede the cheapness issue. It is not unimportant; but economic arguments cannot be the crucial ones . . . . The U.S. government could conceivably raise more money if it farmed out the income tax to private sector. Entrepreneurs in the collection business might well display what one supporter of private prisons claims for their eager operations: "a vitality that is sometimes lacking in civil servants." The degree of vitality would presumably depend upon the likelihood of profit. But once again the idea is unattractive. Encounters with the tax collector would be even more difficult than they are today if we knew that our deductions were also his profit margin. He would be nothing more, in that case, than another competitor, another market antagonist, grasping for our money.

Not an Economic Issue

Private prisons pose similar difficulties but in a much sharper form: for imprisonment, unlike taxation (or conscription), is a way of punishing people, singling out some but not others, not only for painful but also for dishonorable and degrading treatment. How do we ever acquire a right to do that? The question goes to the heart of the state's legitimacy; it is a moral and political—not economic— question . . . .

We can see clearly what is wrong with the private prison. It exposes the prisoners to private or corporate purposes, and it sets them at some distance from the protection of the law. The critical exposure is to profit-taking at the prisoners' expense, and given the conditions under which they live, they are bound to suspect that they are regularly used and exploited. For aren't the purposes of

128

their private jailers different from the purposes of the courts that sent them to jail? All the internal rules and regulations of their imprisonment, the system of discipline and reward, the hundreds of small decisions that shape their daily lives, are open now to a single unanswerable question: Is this punishment or economic calculation, the law or the market?

Petty Tyranny

There are bound to be other questions too, not only about corporate profit-taking but also about private willfulness and caprice. Theorists of free enterprise insist that the market is a disciplinary agent, enforcing rational if not benevolent behavior; but the history of the pre-union factory suggests how ineffective this discipline is at the local level, how much room it leaves for petty tyranny. It is in part because prisoners can't form unions that we, who put them in prison, must accept responsibility for their treatment. How can we teach them their own responsibilities if we evade ours, leaving them to endure what is bound to feel like one more racket?

The Profit Motive

Private operators claim they can build prisons more cheaply. While more efficient administration of construction may reduce costs, the savings are lost to the higher cost of private borrowing, as against public bonds. And, since prison construction is financed through tax shelters, the effect is to narrow the national tax base, shifting the burden of financing jails to our lower-income taxpayers.

What private operators don't mention is the possibility that, once entrenched, they will be able to raise prices with little restraint. Moreover, the cost rises as prison populations grow, since private operators charge a daily fee for each inmate. Public institutions are constrained by their budgets.

Kenneth F. Schoen, *The New York Times*, March 18, 1985.

Even if the market provided some initial control over the treatment of prisoners, it is unlikely to be effective for very long. Once a large private company has built and is operating a number of "facilities," holding thousands of men and women, the state is hardly in a position to break the contract and turn to some upstart entrepreneur with nothing to offer but a bid and a plan. At that point, competition won't do its work: the prison industry will turn out to look very much like the defense industry. This suggests that cost effectiveness may well be a short-term business, but that's not, again, the crucial point. It's more important that cleanliness, safety, and ordinary decency will almost certainly decline over the years. Helpless men and women have never fared well in the hands of profit-seeking entrepreneurs. The incentive system is all wrong. Who will look after the interests of prisoners? Who will be watching the prison owners as they run their "own" business?

Perhaps the courts will be watching. There are already indications that the courts will treat public and private prisons as legally identical institutions. How can they do otherwise? Imprisonment is a state action, and so is every decision made, whoever makes it, about the course and character of imprisonment. All such decisions are subject to constitutional norms, and the courts will do what they can to enforce those norms. The enforcement will probably be more roundabout, and will take longer and be harder to monitor, in private than in public prisons. It is not all that effective now, but at least it offers the hope of legal protection.

Shutting Down Hope

This is probably the chief economic advantage of privatization—that it shuts down this hope, that it offers a (temporary) escape from the enforcement of constitutional norms. The resulting savings are like the profit added when a factory moves from union to non-union territory. If the union catches up, the old situation is restored. Similarly, if the courts catch up, we will find ourselves again where we are now, with judges struggling to do what state legislatures and Congress ought to do—reform the prison system. It will turn out that we haven't privatized the prisons so much as deputized the "owners" and all their employees.

Perhaps, indeed, we should deputize nongovernmental agencies to perform some prison-like functions. The present system is so awful that we all might benefit, prisoners too, from a little flexibility, unorthodoxy, experimentation. But this will have to be the work of nonprofit agencies, with publicly recognized programs and explicit authorization. We should not be contracting out, as if these were not *our* prisoners; we should be bringing new ideas into the orbit of the public service. The argument from democratic theory need not commit us to prisons as they now exist or to a single pattern of bureaucratic organization. The argument commits us only to political responsibility. So long as we send men and women to prison, we have to pay attention to what happens to them once they are there. It may be a sad truth, but it is a truth nonetheless: in a democracy, the prisons belong to the people.

"*Legislatures and commissions have increasingly turned to restitution as a constructive alternative to the severity of imprisonment.*"

Make Criminals Compensate Their Victims

Harvard Law Review

Many people believe that crimes and the punishments for those crimes have become absurdly abstract and unequal. In some societies, a punishment is made to fit a particular crime. In America, trials, judges, and criminal sentencing make punishment far more formal. The author of this viewpoint believes that victim restitution—having the criminal reimburse the victim for the damage he has wrought—helps make punishment more immediate and thus more meaningful. By forcing the offender to recognize the harm the victim has experienced, and by rectifying that harm through reimbursement, restitution both punishes and rehabilitates the criminal. The *Harvard Law Review*, from which this viewpoint is excerpted, is one of the most prestigious and long-standing law reviews in the country. It is written and published by Harvard University law students.

As you read, consider the following questions:

1. How was victim restitution applied in ancient societies, according to the author?
2. How does the author say restitution differs from fines?
3. Why does the author believe that society as a whole benefits from restitution?

"Victim Restitution in the Criminal Process: A Procedural Analysis," *Harvard Law Review*, February 1984. Copyright © 1984, Harvard Law Review Association.

Traditional criminal sanctions have been unsuccessful in furthering the aims of criminal justice. Incarcerating offenders in our overcrowded and expensive prisons fails to rehabilitate the imprisoned or to protect society. Rather than learn how to be productive members of society, prisoners experience abuse and develop values that make them more dangerous to society than they were before confinement. The public has become frustrated with the system of "assembly line justice," through which convicted criminals are placed on parole or probation and are left free to commit further crimes, and with the widespread use of plea bargaining, which diminishes the deterrent effect of criminal sanctions. Growing public dissatisfaction has prompted a wave of innovation: reformers have advocated alternatives such as determinate sentencing, halfway houses, work-release programs, and part-time imprisonment. In their search for new sentencing options, legislatures and commissions have increasingly turned to restitution as a constructive alternative to the severity of imprisonment and the leniency of probation. . . .

Restitution Is Effective Tool

Restitution is an appropriate sentencing tool that effectively promotes the aims of the criminal justice system and therefore necessitates no greater procedural protections than those required by other criminal sanctions. . . .

Restitution has been employed as a punitive sanction throughout history. In ancient societies, before the conceptual separation of civil and criminal law, it was standard practice to require an offender to reimburse the victim or his family for any loss caused by the offense. The primary purpose of such restitution was not to compensate the victim, but to protect the offender from violent retaliation by the victim or the community. It was a means by which the offender could buy back the peace he had broken. . . .

Restitution and Rehabilitation

The rehabilitative value of restitution is recognized by judges who impose restitution because of its impact on the offender and its promotion of correctional aims, by legislatures that authorize restitution as a criminal sanction, and by community service programs that use restitution as a rehabilitative tool. Preliminary research, too, indicates that restitution may be a beneficial corrective device. The sanction's rehabilitative effectiveness stems from its direct relation to the amount of damage suffered by the victim: by ordering restitution, a court forces the defendant to acknowledge in concrete terms the harm he has caused. Because restitution is less restrictive of liberty than is imprisonment, but graver than probation, it bridges the gap between the traditional sentencing alternatives. Furthermore, restitution promotes rehabilitation more effectively than does a fine, because it requires the offender to pay the individual harmed rather than the abstract, impersonal state, and thereby impresses upon the offender his responsibility to others. Through restitution, an offender can express guilt in a socially acceptable manner and can increase his self-respect by gaining a sense of accomplishment.

Like a fine, restitution can also be an effective deterrent. Indeed, restitution may be more effective than a fine. Fines are fixed arbitrarily and unpredictably, often in an amount less than the offender's gain. Restitution, in contrast, more directly corresponds to the loss the offender has caused. For property and white-collar crimes, in which the criminal's gain is usually equal to the victim's loss, restitution provides a particularly effective deterrent.

Restitution Punishes

Restitution also serves the retributive goals of punishment. It is constructed to fit the crime and to emphasize the wrongfulness of the offense and the defendant's moral responsibility. In accordance with a retributive theory of punishment, restitution aims at restoring the relationship between the offender and the victim by making the offender pay for his crime.

Reviving Restitution

Revival of restitution as a criminal sanction serves justice by repairing harm and providing a constructive way for offenders to pay their debts to society. Restitution also supports the rehabilitative aims of modern penology by encouraging the offender to acknowledge and assume responsibility for his act. Its use would help rekindle the confidence of crime victims in a system that historically has treated victims with indifference or disdain (and that has been rewarded with diminishing public cooperation in return).

Robert Abrams, *The New York Times*, August 21, 1984.

In practice as well as in theory, restitution orders—unlike civil damage awards—are specifically geared toward achieving the objectives of the criminal justice system. Many statutes specify that restitution should be ordered only if it will promote deterrence or the offender's rehabilitation. When determining the amount of a restitution order, most courts consider not only the amount of the victim's loss, but also the rehabilitative, deterrent, and retributive effects of the order . . . .

Restitution orders typically reflect judicial concern with rehabilitation. Most courts, recognizing that the frustration of a defendant who is ordered to pay an amount exceeding his financial resources may adversely affect his prospects for rehabilitation, gear the amount of restitution to the offender's ability to pay. Moreover, most courts limit the award to actual damages directly caused by the crime. Pain and suffering, loss of earning capacity, and other unliquidated damages that are particularly susceptible to arbitrary determination are usually not included in a restitution order. Although this limitation results in less than full compensation of the victim, it may well promote the offender's reform. When the defendant believes that the amount of the award is fairly related to the damage he has caused, rehabilitation is more likely . . . .

Restitution Vindicates Society

Restitution permits the court to subdue the anger of society by requiring the offender to pay for the harm he has caused. If the offense is not repugnant or if the damage is disproportionately greater than the defendant's culpability, the court may order less than full compensation.

In sum, restitution is an appropriate and effective criminal sanction that promotes the criminal law's goals of rehabilitation, deterrence, and retribution. Moreover, only within the criminal justice system can restitution foster these aims. Although victims may sue offenders after the state has imposed criminal sanctions other than restitution, society, as well as the victim, has an interest at stake when a crime is committed. Society as a whole may benefit from the correctional effects of requiring the offender to pay money to the victim. But because the victim may not find it worthwhile to pursue a civil action, the public benefits of restitution may be lost if enforcement is left to the victim.

"If the Army's need for men is as desperate as the prisoners' desire to get out of prison, perhaps a kind of symbiotic relation could be developed that would benefit society."

Military Conscription Is a Practical Solution

Jack E. Bynum and Leo C. Downing Jr.

Military conscription of criminals has a long-standing tradition both in the United States and in Europe. During the American Civil War, for example, prisoners on both sides were released to fight. In the following viewpoint, the authors contend that military conscription should again be used as an alternative to prison. They believe that not only would it solve the shortage of military personnel, but also give prisoners a respectable work record that would eventually reintegrate them into civilian society. Jack E. Bynum is a professor of sociology at Oklahoma State University. Leo C. Downing Jr. is a professor at North Georgia College.

As you read, consider the following questions:

1. How are law-abiding citizens twice victimized by criminals, according to the authors?
2. What three problems do the authors believe military conscription could solve?
3. Why, according to the authors, do some argue that it is inhuman to force prisoners to choose between prison and the Army?

Jack E. Bynum and Leo C. Downing Jr., "Military Conscription & War: An Alternative to Prison," *Free Inquiry*, Volume 9, No. 1, May 1981. Reprinted with permission.

A particularly critical current issue related to the United States' war making ability is the debate over military conscription or the civilian draft. . . .

Despite the many complex and serious consequences of war, we conclude that the United States will continue to perceive a need for military preparedness and confrontation in the world arena. . . .

Violent Crimes Serious

Another persistent social problem that demands acknowledgment as a valid indicator of contemporary social conditions is the prevalence of criminal behavior of most types among an ever-growing number of citizens. Regardless of massive efforts to improve law enforcement and to prevent these antisocial forms of deviance, most criminologists agree with available statistical reports that show long-range trends of increasing crime in most categories. The rising rates of violent crimes are especially serious. . . .

There are several serious issues concomitant to dealing with crime in the United States. It is becoming an increasingly heavy financial burden for society to maintain correctional institutions and their ever-growing populations of prisoners. A significant part of the social cost of crime can be ascertained if we think in terms of meeting the needs and sustaining incarcerated felons. . . .

Thus, the law-abiding citizens are twice victimized; first through the direct losses experienced when a crime is perpetrated against them or their community, and second, through the taxes they pay to apprehend, convict, and maintain the criminal during incarceration.

Rehabilitation of Prisoners

A second issue related to our national crime problem revolves around the rehabilitation and reintegration of imprisoned persons into society. Parole and probation are widely used, not only as humanitarian and necessary steps in these processes, but as the logical means to reduce our prison populations and related expenses. The severe economic, occupational and social problems of adjustment encoutered by newly released prisoners are well known. . . .

The success of rehabilitation, parole and probation is questionable. Many members of society feel trapped in an intolerable situation of double jeopardy: either pay for the support of dangerous incarcerated criminals, or risk returning them to our streets. . . .

The two social problems of war and crime, together with their respective issues, can be theoretically joined in a complementary junction. The continuing threat of possible war requires military preparedness and a constant supply of trained manpower. The continuing criminal activity necessitates the incarceration and maintenance of hundreds of thousands of prisoners, most of whom are in the appropriate age range for military service.

National leaders warn repeatedly that the United States' decision to support its armed forces with volunteers has made the Army unable to maintain its strength at an adequate level to meet global commitments. Even the United States' involvement in military operations considered vital to national security does not prompt an adequate surge of volunteers. At the same time, thousands of men with criminal records from federal and state prisons and from civilian life after release from prison have volunteered for military service only to be rejected *because* of their criminal record. Civilian industry has long followed the same practice since employers are

"The state prison is full, the county jail is full. Maybe we could get him to enlist in the Army!"

© Pearson/Rothco

usually unwilling to give a former convict a job. Perhaps the time is ripe for the United States to consider this untapped pool of manpower for military service. If the Army's need for men is as desperate as the prisoners' desire to get out of prison, perhaps a kind of symbiotic relation could be developed that would benefit society with enhanced military security, reduced prison populations, reduced incarceration expenses and taxes, and the opportunity for socially redeeming and constructive employment for many prisoners. . . .

Adults initially consigned to prisons for non-violent crimes such as burglary, theft, and white collar crime, and similar offenders already in prison would be offered the alternative of serving their sentences as professional soldiers in the new military organization. Those convicted of more serious crimes, such as murder, rape, and kidnapping would require more rigorous screening, but it is conceivable that many of them could serve the nation as soldiers in the new military organization.

These troops would be trained and garrisoned at bases remote from the mass of American society like . . . remote desert areas, yet strategically located for rapid military deployment. Strict military discipline and the system of military justice would prevail at these isolated bases.

Benefits to Ex-Prisoners

We have already expanded on the pragmatic advantages to society of a new military force that includes successful assimilating of a significant proportion of persons with criminal backgrounds and paroled convicts. Besides the obvious merit of substituting military service for prison sentences and capital punishment, there are three other benefits to such recruits.

Benefits to Military Conscription

1) *Improved occupational identity.* For the first time in their lives, many of these men, through enlistment in this military organization, would have a socially legitimate occupation and meet the basic needs for food, shelter, clothing and health care. Participants would receive the usual remuneration of American military service personnel of comparable rank, and would have opportunity for advancement. While soldiers do not have the highest social status, they are not socially rejected, as are ex-convicts. It has already been established that work furloughs for prisoners as an alternative to incarceration is positively associated with a reduction in recidivism. We perceive meaningful employment of ex-prisoners in the military as a viable program of rehabilitation.

2) *Improved values and attitudes.* The military experience, in which people must live and work together in close cooperation for the attainment of common objectives should not only develop esprit de corps, but stronger respect in individual members of the group

for the rights and property of others. Certainly, the social and community nature of barracks life opens virtually every aspect of one's life to observation, leaving little room for major deviance from group standards. Even those opposed to the military draft acknowledge that military service teaches discipline, patriotism, and concern for comrades to most recruits. This may be the most valuable kind of resocialization for people with a past record of insensitivity and irresponsibility toward society and the immediate community.

3) *Reintegration into society.* Most prison recruits who satisfactorily fulfill a 5-year enlistment in the "United States Foreign Legion" could be honorably discharged and returned to civilian life in this country. In addition, when a foreign government requests and receives military assistance, it should be understood and agreed that such a government must make full citizenship available at the end of the conflict to those United States troops that fought on behalf of that country. In this way, even those former prisoners who, because of extremely serious crimes, might be denied reintegration in the United States, could find a home and citizenship with honor elsewhere.

Environmental Factors of Crime

We propose that we moderate the sociological determinism that dictates so many programs developed for the prevention and treatment of crime. While much antisocial deviance can be traced directly to the offender's family, neighborhood, poverty, and lack of opportunity in the social environment, by transferring the criminal's guilt to society, we tend to forget and ignore the offender's own responsibility for personal behavior. The focus on society as a total explanation for deviance fails to explain adequately why and how the majority of people living in the same *flawed* social conditions do not also become a criminal threat.

Our proposal to give military training to large numbers of prisoners and substitute them in warfare for more law-abiding citizens, while alleviating many of the problem issues is clearly not a complete or ultimate program for dealing with war and crime. Some argue that it is inhuman to *force* prisoners to choose between a prison sentence and the military service, where they might be injured or killed. But there is ample evidence that many prisoners would prefer military life over prison life. And there is something compelling in the question asked by many members of society: "Why must I be forced through taxation to support a criminal and violent member of a street gang in prison, and either go myself, or send my 19-year old son in response to the military draft to fight in a foreign war?" Other critics will contend that we have failed our national responsibility if, in response to appeals for military assistance from our allies, we send our deviants, misfits, and criminals. But if the situation of our allies is desperate enough to

139

request combat personnel, they will not question the character of the men who take the field in their defense. Finally, since we have been impotent in reducing criminal deviance in the United States, and the heavy social costs of crime victimize all of us, we should be ready to generate, refine, and test more imaginative and more daring approaches.

"To punish him with pain for a few minutes preserves the offender's integrity, and gives him a chance as well to make amends for his crime."

Corporal Punishment Is Effective

Graeme R. Newman

In his book, *Just and Painful*, Graeme R. Newman argues for the use of electric shock and beatings instead of prison. He believes that for punishment to have an effect, it must be short and acutely painful. In the following viewpoint, citing studies in which animals were subjected to electric shocks in order to alter their behavior, Mr. Newman contends that humans would be affected in a similar way. Thus, criminals would be deterred from committing crimes, knowing that the punishment would be severely painful.

As you read, consider the following questions:

1. Why does the author believe that corporal punishment is not being used today in spite of widespread knowledge of its effectiveness?
2. What three reasons does the author give to support his belief that prison is not an effective deterrent?
3. Why is corporal punishment more justifiable than imprisonment, according to Mr. Newman?

Reprinted with permission of The Free Press, a Division of Macmillan, Inc. from *Just and Painful: The Case for the Corporal Punishment of Criminals* by Graeme R. Newman. Copyright © 1983 by Graeme R. Newman.

Many classic experiments on the effects of corporal punishment on dogs, monkeys, pigeons and humans have been conducted in psychology laboratories.

> The gate is opened and the rat dashes along a metal grid. It grabs the food that has been placed at the end of the runway and nibbles it joyfully. Suddenly the rat drops the food, squeals, and springs up in the air, dancing around the edge of the grid as though on hot bricks.
>
> The experimenter has electrified the grid, giving the rat quite a shock.
>
> After a few seconds the shock goes off. The rat sits apprehensively in a corner.
>
> In a couple of minutes the experimenter again drops food into the cage. The rat immediately dashes forward and begins to consume it. Again it squeals, drops the food and dances around, clearly in pain.
>
> The shock goes off. The experimenter repeats the whole procedure again and again. The same thing happens. The rat goes for the food, but drops it when shocked.
>
> Then at about the fifth "trial," as it is called, the rat runs towards the food, but withdraws as soon as it gets near it. After a few times at this, the rat no longer runs toward the food.
>
> Acute corporal punishment has successfully eliminated the temptation to eat food.

Corporal Punishment Works

In a number of similar experiments corporal punishment has been so successful that some animals have starved themselves to death rather than eat the forbidden food. Most studies conducted by psychologists in their laboratories use electric shock when they wish to administer acute pain to their animal subjects.

It is also of interest that the few laboratory studies of the deterrent effects of isolation (that is, the laboratory analogue of prison) have produced much more inconclusive results than have those using corporal punishment. There is little doubt that, in the experimental conditions of the laboratory, acute pain is a very efficient and lasting suppressor of unwanted behavior, both of the person punished (individual deterrence) and of the person watching the punishment (general deterrence).

This is an amazing observation when one considers that the predominant scientific opinion as to whether it is possible to rehabilitate offenders (that is, do something to them to stop them from committing again) is that *nothing works*.

Why is this? It is because those who have reviewed the research on punishment as a deterrent have been biased.

Three Biases of Deterrence Research

1. Researchers have used a different set of standards for evaluating corporal punishment as against prison.
2. They have conveniently overlooked all the research on cor-

poral punishment conducted in the psychology laboratory, and, while this research does not have direct application to humans, it nevertheless is an important guide, just as research on the cancerous effects of drugs on animals is considered an important guide.

3. When researchers have recognized the laboratory research on the effectiveness of punishment, they have ignored the fact that almost all this research has used corporal punishment....

Why Prison Is a Bad Deterrent

1. *Chronic pain is not as efficient as acute pain.* The punishment applied to the subjects of the punishment experiment described is one that is always defined in terms of acute pain. In real criminal punishment, this is far from the case. The punishment is drawn out into long prison terms which are then—almost as an apology for their being long—turned into periods of "humane" punishment, described as deprivation of liberty, while maintaining many physical comforts.

Why Not?

What is needed is a punishment that is severe enough to take a place half way between prison and probation, a space perfectly filled by acute corporal punishment. It could also help to head off those sentences that are characteristically used by juvenile court judges, such as incarceration at a detention center for "assessment" or under some such pretext, or when the sentence of prison is used as a "short sharp shock."

If a short sharp shock is what is needed, why not administer it?

Graeme R. Newman, *Just and Painful*, 1983.

---

2. *Time works against prison.* The scientists of punishment know what makes punishment most effective: it must be immediate and swift. That is, it must be administered as soon after the offense as possible. In that way both the offender and the public are able to make the connection between the crime and the punishment. This important technique of punishment is quite commensurate with retribution, in that, if the link between the punishment and the crime is to be clearly forged, it must occur as close as possible to the crime. Thus, people will see the meaningful connection between the punishment and the crime. The longer the delay the less deserved will seem the punishment.

For example, we find ourselves in great difficulty understanding the justice of punishing an offender who has been, say, in hiding for twenty years leading a life as a productive citizen, who is finally apprehended and sentenced to several years prison for a crime he

143

committed so long ago. Such a punishment seems somehow not right.

Time Makes Prison Ineffective

It may be that it is because all we have to punish with is "time," that the time elapsed since the offense naturally eats away at the punishment. If we were to administer a punishment that was acute and extremely brief, such punishment does not seem so out of place, and is less affected by time. The offender, even though he has spent the last twenty years as a good citizen, still has his price to pay for the original crime. To make him do even two years in prison would seem unnecessarily destructive. To punish him with pain for a few minutes preserves the offender's integrity, and gives him a chance as well to make amends for his crime. The balance between crime and punishment is restored, and as little damage as possible is done in the process.

3. *Prison maximizes uncertainty.* Any criminal worth his salt knows that he can expect to get caught only for a small number of his crimes. There is no certainty of punishment in real life as far as crime is concerned. However, when we are talking about general deterrence—that is, the deterrence by the threat of punishment of those ordinary people who might otherwise commit a crime—this is not so bad. It is likely that most people grossly overestimate the chances of getting caught, so that the "certainty" of the punishment is ensured through the omnipresence of threat.

Certainty means more than simply the chances of getting caught, and in fact one might argue that this is not really what certainty means when it comes to criminal punishment. Certainty also requires that, when a person is found guilty of a crime the punishment will in fact be carried out.

This is the point on which most criminal justice reformers have concentrated their energies over the last few years. They have complained that judges' discretion produced highly unpredictable sentences. Their solution, we have seen, was to argue for the legislation of mandatory or fixed sentences.

Prison Terms Uncertain

This makes the punishment certain all right. But it makes the wrong kind of punishment certain. In fact, these reformers have mixed up certainty with severity. As long as the words "mandatory" or "fixed" are there, they think that the problem of certainty is solved.

It is not, of course.

The only thing that is certain is that the offender will go to prison (that is, if he has not undergone plea bargaining for some lesser offense—although some legislatures have also tried to outlaw plea bargaining in an attempt to ensure certainty of punishment). However, it is *not* certain that he will be punished appropriately, or that the experience of prison will even be painful.

This problem would not arise if prisons were made once again retributive, if the split between the crimes and the criminals was made immense enough.

One final defense of the deterrent use of corporal punishment can be made—this time, paradoxically, from the point of view of retribution.

Corporal Punishment Can Deter Crime

The argument in favor of the acute corporal punishment of criminals would be made easier if it could be shown that it had little lasting effect on the individuals punished. The reason for this is that, according to the principles of the "old retributivists," their main moral defense of punishment is this very fact: that it punishes the act only, and leaves the person unaffected (that is, unchanged). In this sense, the finding that "nothing works" is great support for their position!

Whipping and Electric Shock

Acute corporal punishment should be introduced to fill the gap between the severe punishment of prison and the non-punishment of probation.

For the majority of property crimes, the preferred corporal punishment is that of electric shock because it can be scientifically controlled and calibrated, and is less violent in its application when compared with other corporal punishments such as whipping.

For violent crimes in which the victim was terrified and humiliated, and for which a local community does not wish to incarcerate, a violent corporal punishment should be considered, such as whipping. In these cases, humiliation of the offender is seen as justifiably deserved.

Graeme R. Newman, *Just and Painful*, 1983.

The psychologists who advocate the use of painful techniques to eliminate unwanted behavior argue that their methods are designed specifically to eliminate only the particular unwanted behaviors of the individual and leave the individual's personality essentially untouched. . . .

If we must use deterrence as the standard by which to measure corporal punishment, we may say that not only can it be shown to have a specific deterrent effect on a specific behavior (which cannot be shown for prison) but it also is a more justifiable deterrent in comparison with prison because it focuses on the act rather than the actor.

Distinguishing Bias from Reason

The subjects of prisons and crime often generate great emotional responses in people. When dealing with such a highly controversial subject, many will allow their feelings to dominate their powers of reason. Thus, one of the most important basic thinking skills is the ability to distinguish between opinions based upon emotion or bias and conclusions based upon a rational consideration of the facts.

Most of the following statements are taken from the viewpoints in this chapter. The rest are taken from other sources. Consider each statement carefully. *Mark R for any statement you believe is based on reason or a rational consideration of the facts. Mark B for any statement you believe is based on bias, prejudice or emotion. Mark I for any statement you think is impossible to judge.*

If you are doing this activity as the member of a class or group compare your answers with those of other class or group members. Be able to defend your answers. You may discover that others will come to different conclusions than you. Listening to the rationale others present for their answers may give you valuable insights in distinguishing between bias and reason.

If you are reading this book alone, ask others if they agree with your answers. You too will find this interaction very valuable.

R = a statement based upon reason
B = a statement based on bias
I = a statement impossible to judge

1. If pain is an effective deterrent to laboratory rats, it can be effective for humans.

2. Punishment is most effective when it is immediate and swift.

3. To punish him with pain for a few minutes preserves the offender's integrity, and gives him a chance as well to make amends for his crime.

4. Corporal punishment is a more justifiable deterrent than prison because it focuses on the act rather than the actor.

5. A way of relieving overcrowding in the prisons and at the same time providing the military with enough personnel would be voluntary military conscription for prisoners.

6. Military conscription would give prisoners' legitimate employment status.

7. The two problems of war and crime could both be overcome if military conscription were used instead of prison.

8. Since restitution compensates the victim, it provides a reconciliation between criminal and victim.

9. Helpless men and women have never fared well in the hands of profit-seeking entrepreneurs.

10. Cheapness should not be a prison issue.

11. If prisons are private ventures, there would be less governmental control.

12. Privately-operated prisons can realize significant cost-savings for governments and eliminate a considerable administrative burden as well.

13. Corrections authorities could shop around for the best facility if prisons were run by private firms.

14. Private industry has always been more creative than federal and state industry.

15. Probation has lost effectiveness because it has had too little financial backing.

16. Prison alternatives are failing. The only thing the public can do is provide enough prisons for those that belong there.

17. Those responsible for funding have been unwilling to recognize the seriousness of probation's plight.

18. Statistics can be used to formulate the wrong conclusions.

19. Probation officers' enormous caseloads make probation a sick joke.

Bibliography

The following list of books, periodicals, and pamphlets deals with the subject matter of this chapter.

George M. Anderson	"Probation: Its Unfulfilled Potential," *America*, April 6, 1985.
James Austin	"The Unmet Promise of Alternatives to Incarceration," *Crime and Delinquency*, July 1982.
Richard Behar	"Partners in Crime," *Forbes*, February 11, 1985.
Allen F. Breed	"Don't Throw the Parole Baby Out with the Justice Bath Water," *Federal Probation*, June 1984.
Nick DiSpoldo	"Halfway Houses: A Prison Alternative," *America*, April 20, 1985.
Kevin Krajick	"For Punishment," *Harper's*, April 1984.
National Moratorium on Prison Construction	*Alternatives to Imprisonment*, pamphlet available from 78 Beacon St., Boston MA, 02108.
Joan Petersilia	*Granting Felons Probation*, Santa Monica, CA: The Rand Corporation, 1985.
Prison Research Education Action	*Instead of Prisons*, New York: Syracuse, 1982.
Philip Shenon	"One Price of High Bail: Overcrowded City Prisons," *The New York Times*, November 13, 1984.
E.R. Shipp	"Group Aiding Ex-Convicts Begins Running a Jail," *The New York Times*, February 17, 1985.
Jay Stuller	"Putting Prisons To Work!" *The American Legion*, January 1983.
Daniel Van Ness	"The Crisis of Crowded Prisons," *Eternity*, April 1985.

Organizations to Contact

American Correctional Association
4321 Hartwick Rd.
Suite L208
College Park, MD 20740
(301) 699-7600

A group of administrators, wardens, probation officers and others whose goal is to improve correctional standards. The organization studies causes of crime, juvenile delinquency, and methods of crime control and prevention. They publish *Corrections Today*, a bimonthly newsletter, and other publications.

Association of Programs for Female Offenders
Community Responsibility Center Inc.
New York Building
1651 Kendall St.
Lakewood, CO 80214
(303) 232-4002

The group is dedicated to the improvement of services to female offenders, seeks to stimulate awareness, encourage cooperation in identifying the unique needs of the female offender, and to cross geographical barriers to effectively communicate with all interested individuals, agencies and organizations.

Federal Bureau of Prisons
320 First St. NW
Washington, DC 20534
(202) 724-3198

The bureau publishes materials on the current prison system.

Fortune Society
39 W. 19th St., 7th Fl.
New York, NY 10011
(212) 206-7070

A group of ex-convicts and others interested in penal reform working to create a greater public awareness of the prison system and to understand the problems confronting inmates before, after, and during incarceration The members work on a personal, one-to-one basis with men and women out of prison to help convicts find jobs. It publishes a monthly newsletter.

Friends Outside
116 E. San Luis St.
Salinas, CA 93901
(408) 758-2733

The group provides social services to jail and prison inmates, their families and ex-offenders. Their purposes are: to aid prisoners and their families in overcoming the traumas and limitations imposed by their separation, to assist public officials in improving prison conditions, to aid ex-offenders in making the transition from confinement to freedom, and to develop better community awareness of the problems caused by incarceration. Friends Outside publishes a monthly newsletter.

International Prisoners Aid Association
Department of Sociology
University of Louisville
Louisville, KY 40292
(502) 588-6836

A group of agencies and individuals in forty-five countries concerned with prisoner aid programs. Its purpose is to assist nongovernmental organizations to serve more effectively in their efforts to prevent crime, rehabilitate offenders, stimulate social action and legislation and disseminate worldwide information concerning sound methods of crime control. It publishes a newsletter.

National Center on Institutions and Alternatives
814 N. St. Asaph St.
Alexandria, VA 22314
(703) 684-0373

The center serves as a clearinghouse on decarceration and aids in developing and promoting strategies and actions to reduce the number of people involuntarily institutionalized. It works toward developing, promoting, and supervising enduring alternative programs, and eliminating unnecessary lockup in prisons. It sponsors the Client Specific Planning Program for prisoners. It publishes books and pamphlets, including a monthly newsletter.

National Coalition for Jail Reform
1828 L St. NW
Suite 1200
Washington, DC 20036
(202) 229-7119

The coalition works to reform the nation's jails by educating the public on the unnecessary incarceration of individuals such as the mentally ill and retarded, public inebriates, juveniles and pretrial detainees. It publishes many brochures, position papers and proceedings.

National Council on Crime & Delinquency
77 Maiden Lane
4th Fl.
San Francisco, CA 94108
(415) 956-5651

An organization of social workers, corrections specialists and others
interested in community based programs and the prevention, control, and
treatment of crime and delinquency. The council publishes a multitude
of publications including the monthly *Crime & Delinquency*.

National Institute of Victimology
2333 N. Vernon St.
Arlington, VA 22207
(703) 528-8872

Founded in 1976, the institute works to improve victim/witness services
and to make the public and criminal justice personnel aware of the needs
of crime victims. It publishes a quarterly journal, *Victimology*.

National Moratorium on Prison Construction (NMPC)
309 Pennsylvania Ave. SE
Washington, DC 20003
(202) 547-3633

The moratorium is a project of the Unitarian Universalist Service Committee. NMPC works toward a halt to all prison and jail construction until
alternatives to imprisonment are fully evaluated and implemented. The
Moratorium's newsletter, *Jericho*, is published quarterly.

National Prison Project
1346 Connecticut Ave. NW
Suite 402
Washington, DC 20036
(202) 331-0500

A project of the American Civil Liberties Union established to provide
litigation and education programs aimed at improving prison conditions
and developing alternatives to incarceration.

Offender Aid and Restoration
Historic Albemarle County Jail
409 East High St.
Charlottesville, VA 22901
(804) 295-6196

A community-based movement of volunteers that aid prisoners and ex-
prisoners in making the transition from prison to outside. The organization is also involved in jail reform.

The Police Foundation
Suite 200
1001 22nd St.
Washington, DC 20037
(202) 833-1460

The foundation is a non-profit criminal justice research organization.

Prison Research Education Action Project
Shoreham Depot Rd.
Orwell, VT 05760
(802) 897-7541

A national project of the New York State Council of Churches to provide educational materials which advocate prison abolition and safer, non-repressive alternatives for victims and offenders in a prevention framework. It has published several books and manuals.

Prisoner's Union
1317 Eighteenth St.
San Francisco, CA 94107
(415) 648-2880

A group of convicts, ex-convicts, and others interested in improving conditions of those incarcerated in California prisons. Its goals include seeking redress for convict grievances, ending economic exploitation by gaining the right to a prevailing wage for all work done in prison, establishing a uniform and equitable sentencing procedure, and restoring civil and human rights to convicts and ex-convicts. It publishes *The California Prisoner*.

Volunteers of America (VOA)
3813 N. Causeway Blvd.
Metairie, LA 70002
(504) 837-2652

A national Christian human services organization founded in 1896 to provide material and spiritual assistance to those in need. VOA provides residential pre-release centers for vocational training, counseling and job placement to adult offenders and provides material aid and counseling for families of prison inmates.

Women's Prison Association and Home
110 Second Ave.
New York, NY 10003
(212) 674-1163

The assocation provides temporary shelter and individualized treatment for women and girls who have been in trouble with the law. The group maintains an interest in prison conditions and in legislation regarding women offenders.

Appendix of Periodicals

The following publications deal with the subject of prisons. They have been included because they are unique and not commonly available in public or school libraries.

The Angolite
Louisiana State Penitentiary
Angola, Louisiana 70712
$8 per year.

One of the most well-known of the prison publications, *The Angolite* is written and edited solely by inmates of Angola Prison. It is published six times a year.

The California Prisoner
1317 Eighteenth St.
San Francisco, CA 94107
$15 per year.

Published six times a year for members of the Prisoners Union, the newspaper is devoted exclusively to prison conditions and problems.

Case & Comment
P.O. Box 1951
Rochester, NY 14962
$7.50 per year.

This magazine, published six times a year, analyzes current controversial court cases that affect different aspects of the criminal justice system, including prisons, and includes commentaries on the cases.

Criminal Justice Ethics
Institute of Criminal Justice Ethics
444 West 56th St.
New York, NY 10019
$15 per year.

This magazine is published bi-annually and deals exclusively with ethical issues.

Fortune News
The Fortune Society
229 Park Avenue So.
New York, NY 10003
$10 contribution.

A monthly newspaper published by the Fortune Society, a non-profit organization of ex-convicts and other interested persons. *Fortune News* is published five times a year.

Grapevine
Joint Strategy and Action Committee
475 Riverside Dr.
Room 560
New York, NY 10115
$5 contribution.

Published monthly by the Joint Strategy and Action Committee, which is composed of a coalition of national mission agencies of 16 Protestant denominations, *The Grapevine* regularly devotes issues to criminal justice problems.

Institutions Etc.
814 N. St. Asaph St.
Alexandria, Virginia 22314
$12 per year.

This newsletter is published monthly by the National Center on Institutions and Alternatives, which works toward the abolition of prisons.

Jericho
National Moratorium on Prison Construction
309 Pennsylvania Ave. SE
Washington, DC 20003
$7 per year.

Jericho is published quarterly by the National Moratorium on Prison Construction, a project of the Unitarian Universalist Service Committee (UUSC). The Moratorium works toward a halt to all prison and jail expansion until alternatives to incarceration are fully implemented.

Judges' Journal
American Bar Association
1155 E. 60th St.
Chicago, IL 60637
$15 per year.

The Journal is a quarterly publication of the American Bar Association. They publish many readable articles on the subjects of prison and sentencing reform.

Review of Law and Social Change
New York University
249 Sullivan St.
New York, NY 10012
$12 per year.

The Review is published annually, and each issue takes on a criminal justice topic.

Index

156